MAKE MORE MONEY
INVESTING IN
MULTIUNITS

A Step-by-Step Guide to Profiting from Apartment Buildings

GREGORY D. WARR

Dearborn™
Trade Publishing
A **Kaplan Professional** Company

President, Dearborn Publishing: Roy Lipner
Vice President and Publisher: Cynthia A. Zigmund
Acquisitions Editor: Mary B. Good
Senior Managing Editor: Jack Kiburz
Interior Design: Lucy Jenkins
Cover Design: DePinto Design
Typesetting: Elizabeth Pitts

Published by Dearborn Trade Publishing
A Kaplan Professional Company

Library of Congress Cataloging-in-Publication Data

Warr, Gregory, D.
    Make more money investing in multiunits : a step-by-step guide to profiting from apartment buildings / Gregory D. Warr.
        p.   cm.
    Includes index.
    ISBN 1-4195-0377-4 (7.25 × 9 pbk.)
    1. Real estate investment. 2. Apartment houses.   I. Title.
    HD1382.5.W37   2005
    332.63′243—dc2
                                                                2005003103

Dearborn Trade books are available at special quantity discounts to use for sales promotions, employee premiums, or educational purposes. Please call our Special Sales Department to order or for more information at 800-621-9621, ext. 4444, e-mail trade@dearborn.com, or write to Dearborn Trade Publishing, 30 South Wacker Drive, Suite 2500, Chicago, IL 60606-7481.

I dedicate this book to my family:

To my parents Barbara and Frank
My sister Pam
And to my grandparents Mary and Harold

I'd like to acknowledge the following people:

- My friends and family; too many to list but you have all added to this book in one way or another
- Everyone down on the floor of the exchange, for showing me competition with sportsmanship
- Robert G. Allen, who introduced me to real estate
- Everyone at Dearborn Trade Publishing, especially Mary Good; when things got tough, Mary was right there
- And to Barbara McNichol, Sherry Sterling, and Faye Q. Heimerl, who helped make this book a reality

Over the last few years hundreds of thousands of people have attended Real Estate Investing Boot Camps. Although money can be made and is made in the purchasing and sale of single-family homes, it is a challenging if not insurmountable way to create *long-term wealth*. *How long will it take to become rich from buying one house at a time?* This book is written for those people. Why? Because almost all of those boot camps focus on purchasing single-family homes. My experience tells me the proven way to become wealthy is through investing in apartment buildings (commercial residential real estate)—*not* single-family homes.

There are two main reasons why little has been written on the subject of investing in multiunit real estate. Reason one: Few people know how to invest this way. Reason two: those "in the know" want to keep what they know a secret. This book blasts the second reason wide open! I *want* to share what I know.

With commercial real estate, as with most things in life, it's fairly simple to make money—but it's not easy. But, if you can teach someone to do what you do by following a step-by-step plan, then you have a "system." And with most processes everything becomes easy to remember when you can follow a repeatable system. So naturally, by teaching others how to invest in commercial real estate, I've learned a few things, too. It's a pleasure sharing what I've learned with you.

Where I Come From

I had traded stocks, futures, and options on Wall Street since 1990. I made a lot of money. I lost a lot of money, too. And, I was doing well financially but the emotional ups and downs of the Wall Street world got to me—big time—so I began looking for an area of investment that would bring me stability and satisfaction. I knew people made money in real estate so I decided to buy a single-family house. Then I met a retired police officer who'd been investing successfully for some time. He introduced me to buying apartment buildings. I'd been shying away from buying apartments because I assumed I'd need a lot of cash first, but he was living proof that it doesn't take loads of money to get started. A funny thing happened also; as I began making money in commercial real estate I also started making more money on Wall Street. They work well together as investments but only by using a specific format that I figured out. In this book I will share with you the real estate side of that equation.

What I Offer

I've developed a system that shows you how to create wealth through commercial real estate, and specifically through apartment buildings. I'll start in Chapter 1 by explaining why investing in apartment buildings makes the most sense, and which kinds of apartment buildings best lend themselves to building wealth.

In Chapters 2 and 3 you'll then learn to set a strategy and locate the right property based on that strategy. While you do this, you'll gain lots of ideas for tapping into the expertise of real estate brokers, management companies, and other investors who can help you.

Once you've located properties that look like good investment opportunities you'll need to determine what they're worth. Chapter 4, "Analyzing the Deal," includes a form to keep track of important details about each property that will help you determine its value. In Chapter 5, "Gathering More Details," you'll learn how to determine market rents and income, and expenses.

In Chapter 6, "Using Creative Financing," I explain how to find private funds for your investments instead of using conventional funding sources. In "Structuring the Offer and Negotiating," Chapter 7, you'll access one of my gifts to you: a sample purchase contract. You'll also receive three successful tips for writing a "winning" offer and negotiating on that offer until you get what you want.

When it comes to big-ticket purchases like apartment buildings, it's wise to bring in partners—but how do you deal fairly and profitably with partnerships? Chapter 8 on forming partnerships lays out the best types of partnership possibilities. You'll learn to determine which ones suit you the best.

Chapter 9, "Working with a Team," outlines how to set up your real estate team for optimal results and locate the one team member who can literally guarantee your success, while Chapter 10, "Closing on the Property," explains how to handle inspections and management companies, and includes two killer closing strategies.

Once you own an apartment building, how do you run it? "Managing the Building," Chapter 11, can mean overseeing construction of an apartment building, working with a management company, or renting to federally guaranteed tenants. I'll tell you how to do that and how to multiply your profits while running the property.

I conclude in Chapter 12 with "Putting It All Together," an overall view of buying apartment buildings as investments. In the final chapter, "Giving Back," I'll show you how you can use commercial residential real estate as a charity that can strengthen whole neighborhoods and yourself.

On a radio program recently, I was called "the new breed of investor" because of my extensive background as a trader on Wall

Street (owning a seat on an exchange) and my success in commercial real estate. It seems to have caught on, because programs I go on (TV and radio) and people I talk to now refer to me in this way. I think it is unique, as I'm told that I am the only person at this time who has these credentials, but more important, it helps me because of the strength these two markets share. In this book and through reference material, I will show you how to *Make More Money Investing in Multiunits.*

I know there's a lot to learn, but I'll be with you all the way. I hope you're as eager to make money as I was.

1

WHY INVEST IN APARTMENT BUILDINGS

You may have heard that many wealthy people make money in real estate. When I heard that, the first question I asked was, "What type of real estate?" Most people who have average incomes couldn't answer that question when I asked them, so I set out to find *wealthy* people to ask, "What type of real estate do you own?"

To my amazement, most of the wealthy people I contacted didn't want to take my calls, much less give me an appointment. Where their wealth came from probably wasn't something they'd considered before anyway. Their families taught them what to do, and so they just followed their example.

When I say "wealthy," I'm talking about individuals who have several generations' worth of money supporting them—long-time wealth. I'm not talking about money made within the last year, the last couple of years, or even in one generation. That kind of money makes people rich but not wealthy. A rich person's money might come from a lot of hard work and gallons of sweat, but that doesn't guarantee the money will last. Instead, I looked for people who were considered *recession proof.* I wanted to find out what made their wealth last for generations.

THE DIFFERENCE BETWEEN WEALTHY AND RICH

The distinction between "wealthy" and "rich" became clear to me after my CPA said, "Typically, wealth only lasts one generation." I asked her what she meant. "Well, usually one generation earns all the money and the next generation spends it all." At that point, I realized whom I needed to talk to—the person who came from at least three generations of money. This person would be able to answer my question.

Now, as I said, wealthy people weren't exactly waiting for my call; after all, I wasn't one of them, so why would they want to talk to me? Therefore, I needed to *become one of them,* so they'd feel comfortable enough with me to confide exactly how they made their money in real estate. But how was I going to do that? Did I need to make millions of dollars and live through three generations? It hurt my head just trying to figure out how that would work. I asked: Where do the wealthy congregate? Answer: Charitable events. So I started going to charitable events. Now, these are not casual throw-a-quarter-in-the-bucket events but rather top-of-the-line events—the kinds of occasions with names like The Crystal Ball. Just the names of these events alone make your wallet cower in fear. Although expensive—sometimes $1,000 a plate—I determined that these charitable events were a worthwhile way to spend a night surrounded by some of the wealthiest individuals in New York City. (Besides, the money went to charity. That's what I call a win-win situation.)

What Wealthy People Buy

I was seeking the answer to my question: What type of real estate do wealthy people buy? Although they don't necessarily have the "best" systems for acquiring this type of real estate, clearly they understand how to use real estate to create long-term, passive income. I learned that wealthy people own apartment buildings—specific types of apartment buildings.

The Wealthy Mentality

Most people think running a business means having employees work for them. I like the "wealthy mentality" for running a business better—manage a building, not manage employees. That way, you don't face the interpersonal challenges you'd have with employees. Your piece of property never calls in sick, never asks for a day off, and rarely asks for a raise higher than the rate of inflation.

The wealthy people told me about the type of real estate to buy—apartment buildings—but they didn't tell me how to do that without having a lot of money in reserve. You see, wealthy people have an asset that I didn't have—lots of money. They're able to locate a building and pay cash for it or at least offer a large down payment. I needed to fill the gap between what I wanted to buy and what I could afford. I needed to learn about creative financing, which makes the strategies in this book work.

Think Big

The day I found a mentor—someone who's gone through all the steps and knows how to dodge the landmines investors face—things started to come together for me in real estate.

My mentor is a successful individual who wishes to remain anonymous but doesn't mind if I help you the way he helped me. He told me I needed to "think big" if I planned to make money in real estate. He meant to think big not necessarily by thinking egotistically but by always looking for ways to grow as a person and as a business. That means constantly reevaluating decisions and actions.

I've found efficiency to be closely linked to success. I focus constantly on ways to streamline whatever I'm doing, determining how I can get better results from the same amount of effort. My mentor said, "If you need help, buy it. Buy team members too. You can always find a way to pay for the best."

When it came to what I needed most—money—he said the same thing: "If you want money, just go out and buy it." Now, that advice doesn't seem to make sense, does it? But it makes a lot of sense when you apply it to buying real estate. If I want cash flow (money I make on a regular basis renting out a piece of property), I need to go out and buy a building from which I can get a cash flow. If I want a *small* amount of cash, I buy a *small* building. If I want a *large* amount of cash, I buy a *large* building. This concept is simple, isn't it? Even so, it seemed complex to me at first. *Yet going out and buying money is the core of what I do in real estate.*

My mentor said that when I buy a single-family home, I put up one dollar to make $1.20. That's a 1.20-to-1 ratio, which is good. I realize an even higher leverage when I buy an apartment building, which means I still put up one dollar but get ten dollars in return. That's a 10-to-1 ratio. I call that millionaire buying power.

TWO-PHASE INVESTMENT STRATEGY

Let me talk about the strategy behind my mentor's success—a strategy that you and I can emulate.

The first phase of this strategy is building momentum: that is, buy smaller buildings with investors' funds and then, over time, graduate to buying larger buildings. I don't intend to make a killing initially but instead establish a track record. As I acquire more and more apartment buildings, I get to the point of owning the company that manages my buildings and other buildings. (Read on; I'll explain how I do this in later chapters.)

Managing apartment buildings other than my own can give me a heads-up to an opportunity before it goes on the market. Often, owners of buildings I manage let me know they plan to sell. When the time is right, I help them get the building ready for sale, and then I'll likely purchase it myself.

The next phase (which I haven't yet achieved) begins when I stop acquiring apartment buildings and become the management company for my buildings. This will save me hundreds of thousands of dollars over the years because I'll hire my own employees rather than pay an established management group. It's like putting my real estate investing career on autopilot, because I can sit back and wait for deals to come to me. Plus, because my company is actively managing others' buildings, I stay up on current events in the real estate market. That way, when a deal presents itself, I understand the present market conditions and get a leg up on my competition.

Making Connections

I have benefited from making connections the way my mentor has and so will you. Those connections include bankers and the federal government. Here's how that works: If a property owner or property management group mismanages a building, the party that has the biggest obligation on the building (typically a bank or the federal government) asks a qualified investor/manager—like my mentor—to take over managing that building. He does so successfully. Then the bank or the branch of the federal government responsible for real estate—Housing and Urban Development (HUD)—knows from the new manager (not from the tenants) any problems that stemmed from the way it had been managed previously. HUD rarely owns buildings, so my mentor typically gets a chance to purchase the building at a substantial discount. He knows exactly what he's getting because he's been running the building for 12 to 24 months. Between the first phase of initial acquisitions and the second phase of managing those acquisitions, he has generated a cash flow in the millions.

This strategy comes from an individual who was a retired civil servant. Now he hires his own employees to manage his properties. He's happily semiretired, and he's very wealthy. If this strategy works for my mentor, do you think it'll work for you?

WHY THIS STRATEGY WORKS

In one of our first conversations, my mentor quizzed me by saying: "Suppose you own a single-family home and a ten-unit apartment building. If you have one vacancy in each building, what do you have?"

"I have a 100 percent vacancy in the single-family home and a 10 percent vacancy in the apartment building." My mentor let my words settle. Then the lights went on! *A single-family home without tenants means no money is coming in!* I'd still have to pay taxes, insurance, maintenance, utilities. And I'd have to pay these expenses out of my pocket.

If I own a ten-unit apartment building and one unit becomes vacant, I still have nine other units generating rent. I have money coming in to pay building expenses as well as generate a positive cash flow.

What Is Cash Flow?

In commercial real estate, cash flow is the amount of money you put in your pocket after paying expenses (mortgage included). If this number is positive, it's called positive cash flow. Conversely, if this number is negative, it's called negative cash flow. If it's zero, it's called a *tax deduction*. I go into more detail in Chapter 4, "Analyzing the Deal."

At that split second when "the lights went on," I knew investing in apartment buildings was for me. It meant that even if I had a vacancy, I wouldn't necessarily lose money because I'd have a built-in cushion for error. I liked this business strategy and could see why wealthy people use it.

Optimum Size: 10 to 25 Units

My mentor once said that any investor who wanted a large cash flow should buy at least a 50-unit apartment building. Experience has taught me that buying a 10- to 25-unit apartment building works better. It's not that I disagree with my mentor as much as I've become more aware of what happens throughout the country. In New York City, a 50-unit apartment building is like a starter building. But because I teach people across the nation and see real estate from the West Coast to the East Coast, I've realized that New York is *not* indicative of the rest of the country. I think owning 10- to 25-unit buildings is a formula that works countrywide.

After talking with my mentor about what I've seen, he has come to agree with me on this. I feel pleased that he was willing to learn from me, a quality that's a hallmark of a true champion and one I take to heart—always being open to learning.

Working Up an Investor's Portfolio

When I worked on a loading dock as a young man, I thought $12 an hour was a good wage—and it was then. After I graduated from college, a $12-an-hour job didn't make sense for me anymore; I was qualified for much higher-paying jobs. You deal with the same principle in property ownership. I call it "working up an investor's portfolio."

I know a successful investor who has a large portfolio of properties. He started with a 13-unit building and then worked up to 200-unit properties. As time passed, he realized it wasn't financially worthwhile to continue managing his smaller units, so he sold off the smallest ones. Why not follow his strategy too? Start small and then graduate to bigger and bigger properties. It's like starting with a low-paying job and graduating to high-paying ones.

You can start building your investment portfolio by buying small properties, such as this investor's first 13-unit building. After that, buy his 25-unit and 50-unit properties. From his track record, you know his properties have been well managed and that you'll be making a sound investment.

BANKS PREFER LENDING LOTS OF MONEY

I asked my mentor how I was supposed to come up with the cash to "buy" a large amount of cash in the first place? "First off," he said, "bankers don't want to mess around lending small amounts of money. They want to lend large amounts. Sure, they lend small amounts of money for purchasing single-family homes and this keeps banks going. But they really want to lend large amounts of money to businesses so they can make a healthy profit. You see, a loan officer is no different than a salesperson."

This is how it works. Let's say John is a loan officer at a bank, and his manager tells him he has to lend $10 million (his quota) over the course of the year. If John fills his quota by lending all of that money, he'll likely get a bonus or a raise.

John lends an average of $100,000 to several homebuyers. You can see that it will take a lot of $100,000 transactions to add up to $10 million. But John is hardworking and gets the job done, earning his bonus and raise, but he can't sit back and relax just yet.

Because John did such a great job lending $10 million, he's given a $20-million quota to lend the following year. Once again, John looks for borrowers, and once again he lends all the money he was in charge of. This makes the bank manager happy; he gives John a raise, a bonus, *and* a new quota of $40 million.

Do you think John would be more efficient lending this money in hundred-thousand-dollar increments or in million-dollar increments? The obvious answer is million-dollar increments, if not multi-million-dollar increments—especially if he could lend them to qualified real estate investors. Why borrow $100,000 when $10 million will do?

Types of Properties

Understand that real estate is divided into two types of properties: residential property and commercial property. These definitions are based on how *lenders* look at a property, not how investors look at it. These are clear-cut, universal definitions; they don't fluctuate from city to city, county to county, or state to state.

Let's look at residential property. Lenders define residential property as any building having from one to four units—for example, a single-family residence, a duplex, a triplex, or a fourplex. All of these units are similar in structure and built under a single roof. From the outside, a single-family residence and a fourplex might look the same, but it's what's inside that counts.

The second type of property, according to lenders, is commercial real estate property. The term *commercial real estate*—like many words in the English language—is defined two ways. One is that commercial real estate is property for a "specific business use"—for example, office, strip mall, warehouse, mixed-use, or raw land. Another definition is that commercial real estate is "residential commercial property"—for example, a building with five or more units.

To summarize, residential property consists of one to four units, whereas commercial property is either property for a specific business use or five or more attached residential units. Throughout this book, residential property will refer to commercial residential.

Speaking Your Lender's Language

Why do *you* have to know this stuff? Finance. Know these definitions before you ask for financing and you'll increase your chances of getting what you ask for. You'll be speaking your lender's language, which is always an advantage because it makes the lender feel comfortable dealing with you. Also, if you know how lenders define a property and what they want to see in that property, you can structure your deal with that in mind.

Think about it this way: If you went to a foreign country and didn't speak the language there, you might not be accepted by the natives. More important, though, you wouldn't be able to ask for what you needed—such as directions to the nearest restroom.

Borrower First, Property Second

The lender's language states: If you want to buy a single-family home all the way up to a fourplex, you must qualify for a loan first as an individual. In this case, the lender looks at the borrower first and the property second.

You might have gone through this qualification process when you purchased your own home. You had to provide the following information for your lender: your adjusted gross income, your expenses, your credit rating/FICO score, how long you've been in your present job, copies of your tax returns for the last three years, hair samples, DNA samples, and so forth.

Just as then, lenders want you to qualify for the loan, even though you might be purchasing a fourplex as rental property. Even if you're buying a fourplex that's fully rented to tenants who've lived there ten years and has a waiting list of people wanting to move in, you still have to qualify first. The theory behind this policy: If every tenant suddenly moved out at the same time, thus leaving you without rent money, you still have to be able to pay your mortgage.

Do you notice any flaws in this policy? First, you have to be well off with a good income and good credit to be able to pay for your personal residence *and* your residential property. Second, let's say you have a good income and good credit, but the number of units you can buy will be limited. You can pay for only so much real estate out of your own pocket before you're leveraged out.

Once your lender determines that you have the right income and credit rating, he or she evaluates the property to see if it's a good deal. If it's overpriced or has some problems, you still might not get financing, even though you qualified for it.

Property First, Borrower Second

The reverse is true in commercial real estate. Lenders examine the property first and the borrower second. *For this reason alone, you can see the advantage of buying commercial property over residential property.* This means lenders are more interested in how much money the property brings in—after expenses—than in the prospective buyer's income or credit. Thus, lenders base their decisions on how profitable the building is expected to be over time.

Why is this? It is because commercial property is managed like a business and is therefore viewed by lenders as a business. The best way to explain this is through an exaggerated example. Remember, residential property is made up of one to four units and commercial residential property five or more units.

Say you wanted to purchase a commercial residential apartment building that was listed at $10 million. (Don't let the big numbers scare you off.) If a bank lends you 80 percent of the property purchase price, it's lending you $8 million. ($10 million × 80% = $8 million). A 6 percent interest rate on a 30-year loan would mean a monthly $47,964.04 mortgage payment (in commercial property, it's not called a mortgage but rather *debt service* because it's a debt that has to be serviced or paid).

Now suppose all of your tenants decide to move out on the same day and you're left without any rental income. Would your lender expect you to take on a second or third job to make up your mortgage? Hardly. The lender understands that this building is a business; it's what *you* get your income from. That's why lenders want to be sure the business will *make money* before they lend you money to buy it.

Profitability and Creditworthiness

Lenders have a way of crunching numbers to determine not only if a building will generate enough income to cover its operating expenses and *debt service* (the commercial term for mortgage, as noted), but also if the owner will make a profit from the venture. More accurately, lenders look for a cushion between what's owed on the property and what's earned from it. (I'd say the lenders have your best interest in mind. It's as if they're double-checking your numbers to make sure you get paid too.)

Yes, lenders eventually get around to checking out the investors themselves, but they're mostly concerned with their creditworthiness.

In the commercial real estate realm, a buyer's creditworthiness basically means a "buyer's credibility." Lenders want to make sure that buyers have credibility to pay off their debt. They have already analyzed the property to make sure it generates income and a profit. Next, they examine the buyer's bill-paying record. Does the buyer pay bills on time? If rental income from the building covers expenses with enough cash flow left to pay the debt service, then the remaining question is: Will the investors pay their bills on time?

The good news is that an investor in commercial real estate can have a lower credit rating than can an investor in residential real estate and still be eligible for a loan. This is because lenders *expect* business owners to have a few "dings" on their credit report—which isn't necessarily looked at as bad but instead as a natural reflection of what happens when business owners use borrowed money.

BUSINESS USE OF MONEY

Let's look into this further. Business owners need to keep money moving in order to keep making more money. It's a basic law in business: If you're not using money, you're losing it. Successful business owners understand this and aren't afraid to borrow money to make more money—so long as they earn more money than they've borrowed. As an example, let's say that I borrow money at 9 percent interest, which means I'm charged 9 percent per year to use that money. Well, in the course of the year that money earns 26 percent. I succeeded in borrowing money cheap. I pay the lender 9 percent and still have 17 percent left over (26 percent earnings – 9 percent interest = 17 percent profit). What is business about, if not profit?

However, borrowing that money cost me more than 9 percent interest. I also had the collateral cost (secondary cost) of adjusting my credit score down in exchange for the ability to borrow that money.

A businessperson thinks: What good is having an 800 credit score if I don't use any credit? I'd much rather have a 680 score, own 400 units, and have a $1 million equity line of credit (the ability to borrow up to $1 million against a business or piece of property) than have an 800 score and nothing to show for it. Let me state this again: "Use it or lose it."

When it comes to creditworthiness, lenders not only want to know if you're borrowing money but also if you're paying it back. If you are, your business is making a profit—and banks like to lend money to profitable business owners.

Here's the bonus. Dealing with commercial real estate, you can actually "borrow" someone else's stellar track record or credit in the industry by hiring a respected management company that already has an established credit record. A management company collects rents, maintains the property, keeps records, and deals with any legal issues that arise. What's left over from rents after covering management salaries and expenses belongs to you, the investor.

In order to help you achieve your real estate goals as quickly as possible, I have put together two Web sites: http://www.Large RealEstate.com and http://www.GregWarr.com.

The first is a reference Web site and contains resources for you in the form of important Web addresses, contacts, and forms. Throughout the book I'll be giving you information for government, public, and private Web sites. There are too many sites that are necessary to my real estate investing strategy to include in this book. However, I will give you two here and list the rest on my Web site.

The second Web site provides real estate content such as new real estate strategies and new ways of financing projects. Because I frequently appear on TV and radio, any scheduled appearances will be listed on this site.

Information is important, and without this information I know your job would be much more difficult, so please accept this as a gift from me to you. Your gift to me will be applying this information and changing your life forever.

BUY PROPERTIES IN HIGH DEMAND

Because it's preferable to buy commercial residential property over residential property, next consider what kind of housing you want to target for investing.

I recommend targeting middle- to low-income (affordable) housing. My reason is simple—more people are looking for middle- to low-income housing than are looking for high-income housing. I also recommend targeting such housing because the federal government offers grants and low-interest loans to investors to provide middle- to low-income housing. Most communities desperately need housing for people who rely on government assistance; the government pays rent subsidies to provide this housing.

When I talk about middle- to low-income property, I'm not talking about apartment property in high crime areas—also known as "war zones." I'm talking about property in safe areas where people work hard yet don't meet the median income (average income for the area). Typically, middle- to low-income commercial properties don't have concierge service, a swimming pool, or beautiful landscaping; instead, they're well-maintained, bare-bones apartment buildings. Tenants like living in them so much that they're often willing to get a second or third job to afford to stay in them.

These high-demand properties can generate large cash flows for investors. Their relatively low purchase price combined with their middle-range rental income makes this combination lucrative for any investment business. Can you see why lenders show interest in lending money for purchasing these types of properties?

Just know that the high demand for these types of rental properties ensures they will command a constant cash flow and, ultimately, wealth for investors like you. In the chapters that follow, you'll see more reasons these types of properties make financial sense.

2

SETTING THE
LOCATION STRATEGY

f you've seen the movie *Trading Places* with actors Dan Ackroyd and Eddie Murphy, you'll probably remember their yelling as they stood in the pit trading stock futures and contracts.

That's what I did for four years as a pit trader on Wall Street. I was on the floor, making good money, losing good money. That's the way it goes down there. The 30-by-30-foot pit holds up to 300 people on a busy day. Normally, about 150 traders are in it, and the shouting gets so loud that no one can hear a phone ring. In fact, the phones used by traders to call in orders around the pits have lights on them so traders can *see* the phones ringing.

One day, I was jostling for position in the pit with about 200 other traders. It had been a long week of the market—and my capital—going up and down. I got frustrated. It was the kind of frustration you might feel when you can't move left or right, forward or backward—but you sure can't stay where you are. I looked around at the other traders and started to believe the grass must be greener for them. I figured they regularly made money hand over fist and were having the time of their life. Meanwhile, I'm riding a financial roller coaster, sometimes making a lot of money and other times losing a lot.

That's the day my frustration boiled over. I said in a normal tone, which, compared to the roar of the trading crowd, constituted a whisper: "I'm sick of taking ten steps forward and nine steps backward." To my amazement, 20 people standing around turned to me and, all in their own way, agreed with what I said. Some gave just a nod, some a high five, and some actually *said* they agreed with me. This all came from the people I thought were doing well financially—people who had stood in the pit *for 20 years*. Yet we all felt the same frustration.

I realized then that if *experienced* traders felt this way, I'd better do something about it or in 20 years, I'd still feel frustrated. That's exactly what I *didn't* want. And that's exactly the moment I decided to get into real estate.

THE CASH COW CALLED REAL ESTATE

I knew a trader on the floor who purchased real estate whenever he made any significant amounts of money. He didn't have much of a plan. He bought everything from vacant lots to delis to farmland to fourplexes. But one thing stood out; whenever he needed funds, he could always turn to his real estate investments and sell one or two of them. For him, real estate was a cash cow. I found that amazing. I kept that information in the back of my mind as I watched him over four years. Then, all of a sudden it made perfect sense: I needed to get into real estate.

Now, don't get me wrong. I loved trading. And I still do. In fact, I continue to own a seat on the New York Stock Exchange. It was my love of trading that got me into real estate. My objective was to get one or two pieces of real estate to bring in money the way the other trader did, so I wouldn't have to rely on making money every day from my trading.

Society has trained us to go out and earn a day's pay for a day's work. One of the toughest things for a trader to do is spend a day at the Exchange without making any money, so many of them do what's called "blowing out." This means losing all of their money in the financial markets because they just can't stay out of the markets when they're not supposed to be there.

Traders sometimes try to "force the trade," meaning they know nothing is going on in the market and it's therefore a dangerous time to be active—but they can't help themselves. It's not because of an addiction; it's because convention dictates that traders (myself included) need to be doing *something*.

So I analyzed my trading and found that 20 percent of my trades were successful. In fact, I knew they'd be successful the moment I put them on the Exchange. Of the remaining 80 percent of my trades, half were up $1,000, down $1,000, up $5,000, down $5,000—basically, a wash, which is expected in trading.

My problem came from that remaining 40 percent—the portion that "does in" the undisciplined traders. It's because they know they shouldn't be in the market when nothing is going on, but they trade anyway. They can feel it, taste it, and sense it—they're not supposed to be making trades in there but believe they should be doing *something*.

Because of that, a lot of conversations go something like this: "What trades do you have on?" The trader responds, "I have a position on XYZ. I'm not that comfortable with it, but if it doesn't do anything in next couple of days, I'll get rid of it." Almost always, that trade becomes a massive loser within a couple of hours after such a conversation.

Noting this, I realized that I needed to keep trading only the 20 percent of the trades that were successful and find another activity to occupy my time. As you can see, I selected investing in real estate. Little did I know how well I'd flourish in this new business.

LOOKING FOR A VIABLE SYSTEM

When I decided to get into real estate, I needed to learn how to invest from somebody who'd done it before. I was looking for an investor who had a fail-safe system. I thought, "If I can do a certain activity but can't turn it into a system that can be duplicated over and over, it's not worth doing—whether it's trading in the financial markets or purchasing real estate."

I went to a bookstore to read up on real estate investing. I picked up a book titled *Nothing Down for the '90s* by Robert (Bob) Allen. (His latest edition is called *Nothing Down for the 2000s.*) That book changed my life. In fact, if you happen to have the book, just look on the back cover.

Bob wrote about real estate and how he challenged himself and others to invest well. He'd put together a system to guide people in meeting those challenges. I enjoyed Bob's approach to creative financing, because—like everybody else out there—I was asking, "How am I going to go out and buy *enough* real estate to bring in the money I need if I don't have millions of dollars to start with?" Bob's creative strategies blew my mind because, as a financial trader, I constantly dissected the markets to discover formulas hidden in all those stock charts. In that milieu, I felt like a duck in water.

Bob talked about buying single-family homes, so I started my real estate venture by purchasing a single-family home. I live on the Upper East Side of New York City where single-family homes are called brownstones because of the brown stone they're made of. (The rest of the country calls this type of building a townhouse.) The New York brownstones are four stories high; some even have elevators. In 2000, they were priced from $3 million to $10 million.

Can you recognize my initial challenge? I didn't think I'd be able to flip (buy a piece of property and sell it quickly for profit) a $3.5 million home or even rent it out for cash flow. I immediately became frustrated, and frustration quickly turned into dejection and self-pity. But I soon ended the self-pity and decided to expand my search.

Strategy for **F**ourplex **S**tructures

As a side note, while I was working on these fourplexes, I developed a phenomenal strategy for building wealth quickly from scratch, a strategy based on the fourplex structure. Because this book is about commercial property, I won't go into detail here, but you can go to my Web site, http://www.GregWarr.com, and download a free report on how to follow my system.

While searching in Brooklyn, I noticed something interesting: A fourplex didn't cost much more than a single-family home—the difference between $225,000 for a single-family home and $285,000 to $325,000 for a fourplex was small. This was amazing. Remember, the disadvantage of a single-family home is that one tenant pays rent whereas the four-family home provides rents from *four* tenants to cover my expenses.

I did the math and decided to become King of the Four-Families. Before I could buy my first four-family home, though, someone introduced me to a six-family unit, and, of course, buying that commercial residential property simply made more sense percentagewise. But before I could close on that six-family unit, I came across a ten-family unit. The rest is, as they say, history.

FINDING YOUR IDEAL PROPERTIES

How do you accomplish in two hours what originally took me six months to figure out? How do you map out a way to find your ideal property?

First, figure out exactly where you are. It's similar to walking into a mall and looking at the map with the spot that announces You Are Here. You need to make your own You-Are-Here maps, so start by buying three maps: one for the city in which you live, one for the county in which you live, and one for the state in which you live. On the city map, pinpoint exactly where you're located (that is, your house) and place a small red dot there. Now lay a penny (or a protractor) over the location of your house on the map and draw a circle around it. Then lay a quarter over your first penny-sized circle, drawing a circle around it. Then put a jelly jar lid over that circle and draw another one. Keep drawing larger and larger circles.

Next, take your county map and do the same thing. Locate where you are and draw three, four, or five concentric circles around that location. Last, take your state map and do the same thing. In this way, you're breaking down the area in which you will locate properties, which gives you a scientific approach that can be duplicated over and over.

Locate 10- to 25-Unit Buildings

Start from where you are (your home) and look at properties within the closest circle. If you don't find the properties you're looking for in that circle (in Chapter 3, you'll learn exactly the type of properties to look for, but for now understand that you're looking for 10- to 25-unit apartment buildings), then expand outward to your next circle. From there, you can go to your county map and then to your state map.

Ideally, you're locating properties as close to your home as possible because you can easily travel to these properties. As you become more successful, you can seek lots of deals across the country, but when you first put together a track record and want to build momentum, stay close to home without adding more variables to the equation. Your goal is to find middle- to low-income properties within these circles.

Locate Blue-Collar Areas

Owning property in a middle- to low-income neighborhood means owning property in a neighborhood of people making below the average for that area and who will occupy the building you buy. That requires looking in middle- to low-income areas (not war zones or high-drug, high-crime areas but blue-collar areas). People who live in these neighborhoods have jobs and a strong sense of community and ownership.

When I started to look at fourplexes in Brooklyn, I didn't know much about middle- to low-income targets at the time; I just saw that the houses in Brooklyn were cheap. A short time after that, my mentor asked me, "What type of properties do you want to buy?"

"I want to do what you do—buy apartment buildings."

"Good. Where do you want to buy them?"

"In midtown Manhattan." (If you're not familiar with midtown Manhattan, it's one of the—if not *the*–premier locations for investment property.)

"Good. How much will those units rent for?"

"I want to rent them out for $10,000 a unit a month." If you just dropped the book, please know that this price isn't far-fetched in New York City, especially in downtown Manhattan.

"Okay, who would rent those apartments from you?" he asked.

"I imagine attorneys or people in marketing or even Wall Streeters."

"If they're not attorneys themselves, do you think they might have friends who are?"

"There's a good chance of that."

"If, for some reason, they didn't want to pay rent, do you think they would find a way not to pay it or ask their attorney friends to help them? Besides, if they didn't want to pay you the $10,000 rent or stay in your unit, do they have other rental options available?"

"Yes. Lots of them."

That's when he told me to consider buying middle- to low-income properties where blue-collar, hard-working individuals live. If these honest people don't have enough money to pay their rent, they go out and get a second or a third job so they *can* pay it. Most likely, they wouldn't have lawyer friends or others to help in paying the rent. They care about their families and find a way to pay because they don't want to be evicted.

He concluded by saying, "Take this advice seriously and realize that you'd be helping people who don't have many alternatives to living there."

Gather Statistics on Median Incomes

Before buying any property, determine what the median income is in different areas. The federal government has taken the time, money, and resources to compile statistics. Understanding them will dramatically help you in real estate.

To find the data you want, do the following:

- Go to http://www.census.gov.
- Then click on the map of the United States on the right-hand side.
- Click the state you're interested in finding information about. (You can break it down further into counties and even cities.)
- You'll see the median income for the state, then the counties and cities.
- Highlight these target areas on your maps.

For more Web sites related to this, go to my site http://www.LargeRealEstate.com.

With that information in hand, you can determine where people who make below-average income are located. And if you were to leave it at this, you would still have 100 times more information than you had when you started. But read on; it gets even better.

SEEK EMPOWERMENT ZONES

The federal government has identified certain areas—called Empowerment Zones—in which to invest money for raising the standard of living in those areas. Some of them have never been developed; others have been hit by hurricanes, tornados, or flooding; still others became dilapidated after industries pulled out. These areas have not only become eyesores, they've become financial problems.

You see, all levels of government are financed by taxes. Your property taxes go toward supporting your community's infrastructure: police officers and firefighters, community upgrades like neighborhood parks, and city and state operations. If a particular area doesn't have houses or businesses from which to generate taxes, that area becomes a financial drain.

The federal government puts money into building up these areas enough to provide a tax base. (Just as my mentor said, "Life is simple. If you want something, go buy it.") That means the government is spending money now to generate more later.

The government started incentive programs in these Empowerment Zones, with most of the funding coming from Community Block Redevelopment Programs. Some programs encourage home improvements and upgrades, such as a new roof, a new boiler, and new windows. (Each city and state is different.) Wouldn't it be great to buy an apartment building and receive federal money to help pay for it or fix it up while providing tax advantages at the same time?

Tax Advantages to Owners

But why would the government give apartment building owners a tax advantage when the reason for building up an area was to *bring in* more taxes? Let me explain.

Say you buy a 100-unit building and then rehab it using your own or investors' money and some federal government money. Then you rent the units to people whose rent payments are made by the federal government through a Section 8 program. In effect, the government also reduces, if not wipes out, your property taxes for that building for 1 to 20 years.

Let's say that, on average, two people per unit live in this 100-unit building. That's 200 people who will be paying taxes on money they've earned. For the convenience of 200 people in that building, it might be advantageous for entrepreneurs to put in a deli, a coin-operated laundry, or a nail salon across the street. The business owners pay taxes on the income they bring in. Then more investors come along and build residential housing. And with more residential housing come more businesses and more tax revenues. See how it multiplies? I recommend you investigate Empowerment Zones as good locations for finding apartment buildings to buy as an investor.

How to Find Information

There are three ways to find information about Empowerment Zones:

1. You can pay me, Greg Warr, about $10,000 and I'll tell you. (Of course, I suggest this.)
2. You can go to http://www.hud.gov.
3. You can call your local HUD office and ask about areas for Community Development Block Grants. Highlight them on your maps and note within which circles they lie.

Also ask HUD where the highest need for Section 8 housing is as well. People whose median income is below the average have a hard time paying rent. They can apply to the federal government for a rent subsidy, which means that if the market rent for a one-bedroom apartment in an area is $500 but renters can afford only $300, those renters can apply for a subsidy to cover the balance—in this case, $200. Remember, this subsidy is *guaranteed* by the federal government. That means that a $200 subsidy is guaranteed to come to you from the federal government. I call this money in the bank.

Find out where there's a shortage of Section 8 housing and target that area for your property search.

HUD isn't the only organization with tenant subsidies, although it might be the largest. My Web site, http://www.Large RealEstate.com, will give you some other alternatives, which is always good because these organizations compete to house tenants and therefore may pay higher rents.

HUD Subsidies

How does HUD determine the amount of someone's rent subsidy? First it determines how much monthly rent an individual can afford. This might be 30 percent of the individual's annual income divided by 12. For example, an eligible Section 8 tenant earns $12,000 a year. Thirty percent of $12,000 is $3,600. Divide this by 12 months and you know the individual can afford to pay $300 a month for rent. HUD makes up the difference. If this individual's rent is $500 a month, the federal government grants a $200 subsidy through the HUD program—40 percent of the rent—and the individual contributes the other 60 percent.

I recommend that you rent to individuals who put up at least 40 to 60 percent of their rent. Why? Because those who use their own hard-earned money to pay their rent tend to have more respect for your building and will take better care of the unit than those whose rents are completely subsidized.

Section 8 Subsidies

When I got started in this business, I talked to a friend in Philadelphia named Lisa who used to run a nonprofit organization that did exactly what I just described. (Please note that this strategy can be used by both for-profit and nonprofit companies. Chapter 13 explains how a nonprofit organization uses real estate to provide services for people in transition.)

Lisa explained the subsidies to me, just as I am explaining them to you. When she asked why I was interested in these programs, I told her I had received a letter from the Housing Preservation and Development (HPD) agency saying if I were interested in renting out units to Section 8 tenants, HPD would send tenants to my property. The agency listed the amount of rent it would subsidize, from which I learned that HPD was willing to pay equal to, if not a hair above, market rent.

HPD is a state organization corresponding to HUD for the federal government. (Check with your state government to find out the name of the program available in your state.) Both can issue Section 8 subsidies, which is beneficial for apartment owners because these owners compete with each other for tenants. With competition, the government might have to pay higher and higher subsidies for rental units.

I called HPD and asked a representative, "I heard that you'll send tenants over to rent apartments in my building. What do you mean by that?"

"You tell me what you have available—a one-bedroom, two-bedroom, or three-bedroom unit, and I'll send over ten potential tenants. You can interview them and choose which ones you like."

"What happens if I don't like any of them?"

"I'll send over ten more."

"What if I don't like those ten?"

"I'll send over ten more."

"So you have a long waiting list."

"That's right."

That convinced me to get started as an owner catering to Section 8 tenants. Lisa told me there are more Section 8 units in Philadelphia than there are tenants, so landlords have to accept below-market rents if they want to accept Section 8 tenants at all. Why would they do that? Because the payments (rents) are guaranteed by the federal government. "But," Lisa explained, "when there's a waiting list, HPD will probably pay above-market rent. Take advantage of it." And that's exactly what I did. When you call HUD about Community Block Development Grants, also find out if there's a tenants' waiting list for Section 8 apartments.

RIDE THE WAVE OF ECONOMIC MOMENTUM

Now that you've put together your map of the area in which you live, found the median income for the area, learned where most of those people live, and targeted areas that the federal government wants to invest in, it's time to see the actual locations.

Visit areas you've highlighted that meet your criteria and are in Economic Development Zones. If your income and Zone locations don't overlap, go to both locations anyway. Remember, there's no right or wrong; just aim to ride the wave of economic momentum. You simply don't want to take a hit-or-miss approach.

Watch Out for the Undertow

Consider this example: If you've swum in the ocean, you're probably aware of undertow. If you're caught in an undertow, the current underneath the water's surface drags you out to sea, and you have little control over it. It's nearly impossible to swim against it; most people drown trying. What you *can do* is swim parallel to shore until you're free from that undertow.

Swimmers fighting the undertow exemplify how most people attempt to invest in real estate. They walk into the water and hope the current takes them where they want to go. When it doesn't, they need to make some kind of adjustment, such as swimming parallel to shore. They end up expending a lot of energy and wasting a lot of vacation time trying not to drown. In real estate, that constitutes wasted effort, wasted years of real estate depreciation, and lost money while just trying to break even.

Surf When Waves Are High

By contrast, riding the wave means creating momentum by catching that killer wave back into shore. Surfers know about this; they don't waste their time going out in water that's flat. They read the *Farmer's Almanac*, they know about tides, and they understand seasonality. They hit the water at the most opportune time—when the waves are at their highest.

So when you find an Empowerment Zone within a mean-and median- income area that's inside of one of your circles, surf's up, dude! Catch the momentum and ride the wave.

Your momentum is (or will be) based on your investment track record. You entice banks to work with you because of a good track record as you catch the wave of economic momentum in areas with *forced appreciation*. Forced appreciation means that you not only rehabilitate a property and push its value up, but you go into areas that the federal government wants to improve quickly. It's the opposite of regular appreciation, which is based on waiting for time to pass to realize an increase in the value of your property.

WHAT TO LOOK FOR IN TARGET AREAS

Start your search in Empowerment Zones in the areas you've selected. Ideally, they are properties where middle- to low-income tenants live.

Here's what to look for:

- Clean buildings and streets
- Graffiti (obviously you don't want graffiti on your property)
- Vacant streets (If you're driving around in the middle of a workday and the streets seem empty, don't get turned off. This is usually a good sign; it probably means residents are away at work.)

B e w a r e   o f   C h a l l e n g e d   Z o n e s

If you drive through the neighborhood and see a lot of trash, disabled vehicles, graffiti, and people wandering the streets at 1:00 PM, you're probably in an *economically challenged zone* (also called a battle zone). I believe in helping people as much as possible, but if I bought a building in such an area, within a short time it would be covered in trash and graffiti that would scare away potential renters. This type of area indicates I can't make money with this property and can't buy more property, which means I can't help more people.

There's only so much that can be done in economically challenged zones. In fact, it's better if one of two things happens: the federal government intervenes by rehabbing the area, or a real estate developer buys up the whole area and rehabs it all.

Also look for:

- Signs of pride of ownership; although residents rent their apartments, they still keep their environment clean and safe.
- Residents who are willing to talk about their neighborhood, especially kids, because they usually blurt out the truth. Not only do I ask them if they like the area, but, most important, I ask them what they don't like about the area or what they would like to change. (You'd be surprised how many people say they love where they live and wouldn't change much about it. If you investigate well, you'll find this is the case most of the time.)
- Indications of safety and cleanliness: "Clean" requires spending money; "safe" requires talking to the local police. Make sure the police you contact know you have an interest in the area. It only takes a policeman circling around the block once or twice more a day to keep a place relatively safe and free from drug use and crime.

ENSURE ACCESSIBILITY OF SERVICES

Once you understand the makeup of an area, look at one more aspect: accessibility to services. Make sure there are necessities—public transportation and shopping centers with strong anchor stores—in close proximity to the property you want to purchase.

Strong anchor stores (or anchor tenants as they are sometimes called) are Wal-Mart, Kmart, Dunkin' Donuts, McDonald's, supermarkets, and major gas stations. They are called anchors because they're part of big corporations that spend millions of dollars doing research and locating *prime* property after which they spend hundreds of thousands of dollars to brand their companies. Notice how every McDonald's looks identical and every Dunkin' Donuts uses the same colors? Companies invest a lot of money into everything that goes with branding. Because of that investment, it's not likely they'll pick up and leave.

Once you've located the anchor tenants in any nearby malls, make sure there are filler stores located between them. Fillers are mom-and-pop stores such as coin-operated laundries, nail salons, hardware stores, delis, and barber shops. These small, locally owned stores provide great community support.

Another filler—storage facilities—are also great to have close by because tenants have a way of accumulating a lot of stuff, and you don't want it all stored in your building. You can either make a discount arrangement for your tenants to use a certain storage facility or, as many entrepreneurs have done, open *your own* storage facility.

EXPAND YOUR REACH

Let's say you want to invest in an area called Smithtown, and you live in Jonestown, which is more than a two-hour drive away. I suggest you find city and county maps of Smithtown, draw your circles, and collect the mean and median income data and Economic Development Zones for those areas circled on the map. Then drive around those areas and again collect data about anchor and filler stores. If you're traveling that distance to buy a piece of property, make sure you're getting into a target-rich area. Just as a surfer can wait a few days to catch a big wave, a lot of momentum (meaning a lot of opportunity) comes when they wait.

While doing your research, you might want to look for a place to relocate in the area. If the market is as hot as you expect, then you'll buy two or three apartment buildings within the next couple of years and possibly open an office there. With enough activity, you could even relocate your family or buy a second home nearby in Smithtown, so you can ride the waves more conveniently.

McDonald's Real Estate History

One of the most important retail anchors is McDonald's. Few people know its history beyond "99 billion served," but its real estate history is important to understand and use as a model.

McDonald's was started by two brothers whose last name was McDonald, of course. Ray Kroc—a real estate developer—started the McDonald's franchise because he wanted to buy a business that he could license to individual entrepreneurs. That way he could acquire more and more real estate but have other people pay for it.

He found the McDonald brothers' restaurant, bought it, and put his plan into motion. He located a prime piece of real estate and built a McDonald's restaurant on it. Then he leased this restaurant to a franchise owner. That franchise lease paid for the physical structure, the franchise rights, and costs on the land. In this arrangement, Ray Kroc kept the franchise fee *and* ownership of the land.

You see, McDonald's is more concerned about buying real estate than frying hamburgers. Based on its track record, within ten years, the real estate that the McDonald's Corporation owns should be worth 10 to 20 times more than its purchase price. What does that mean to you? You've learned that wherever there's a McDonald's, property values are sure to increase. That makes it a good area for you to invest in.

3

LOCATING THE
RIGHT PROPERTY

When it comes to locating properties to buy, I start with the old standby: call from newspaper ads placed by commercial real estate brokers. This approach differs from locating for-sale-by-owner (FSBO) *residential* properties when it's often preferable to directly contact the owner.

Commercial real estate brokers gather information about buildings that are for sale and then accurately communicate that information to investors like you, so you can calculate a building's worth. Remember, your job as an investor is to run a business using real estate as the vehicle. If you spend too much time gathering information yourself, you risk being an ineffective business owner. After all, you make money by buying profitable buildings, not by gathering data.

SHOULD YOU BUY FROM AN OWNER OR BROKER?

There are good and bad factors involved in buying FSBO properties. FSBO signs tip me off that there might be problems with the property: a re-tarred roof instead of replaced roof, an inadequate number of smoke detectors, or a poor track record on maintaining boilers.

D o n ' t   T o u c h   T h i s   **FSBO**!

I once learned about an FSBO property and decided to talk to the owner. When I got to his place at 8:00 AM, it smelled like a brewery. I could see he'd begun fixing up the building, but its siding needed to be sandblasted and painted and its dilapidated awnings replaced. This neglect resulted in poor curb appeal—a strike against him from the start.

As we walked down the basement stairs to get to the owner's workshop, the owner warned me that a woman was living in the doorway of the boiler room. "I don't have the heart to kick her out," he said. The woman, a former model, was 86 years old and sleeping in a beach chair—naked.

Next, I saw that the owner kept his handwritten accounting records in a disorderly notebook. After I asked a few questions, I realized he really didn't even know how much rent his tenants had paid. He was asking $1 million for the property; I knew after some cosmetic work it could easily be worth $2 million, but I dropped the whole idea of buying when he became belligerent after I asked a few questions. This owner really needed a broker to represent his interests—*he* certainly wasn't doing a good job!

Let's say I'm an FSBO seller who's spending all my time compiling property information, placing ads in the newspaper, and showing and managing my building. It's likely I'm cutting corners to save money. If my goal is saving money rather than efficiently running my building and treating it like the valuable assist it is, then buyers had better beware. You can assume I've left a lot of maintenance undone. The quality of the property is in jeopardy.

On the other hand, it's a good sign that the property is valuable if a seller works with a commercial real estate broker. This is because the seller understands that an income property needs to produce an income even while on the market, and that means the property must be maintained. (This information becomes clearer as I review how to analyze the numbers in Chapter 4.)

An added benefit of using commercial real estate brokers is being able to use the fees you pay brokers as deductions on your taxes.

FINDING THE RIGHT BROKER

In Chapter 2, you learned to draw concentric circles on a city, county, or state map to help you define the target areas in which you want to invest. Then you learned how to locate Empowerment Zones by contacting HUD. Now, you'll want to locate professionals in your target area who can help you—real estate brokers, management companies, and investors.

Drive around your target area again. Before, you had simply checked out neighborhoods; now you're looking for For Sale signs on commercial buildings. These signs list the brokers representing the sale. Write down their names and contact numbers; also jot down all brokers' names you see on signs for residential properties. You want to know all the "players" in your target area.

Next, interview all those brokers you've identified. You're looking for an aggressive broker to work with, one who knows the area well and understands Section 8 housing. A nonaggressive broker might say, "I don't deal in that area," whereas an aggressive broker will make it a point to deal there and find exactly the properties you're looking for. Aggressive brokers quickly respond to your questions and scramble to retrieve whatever data you ask for. They willingly do whatever work is necessary—and don't waste your time socializing. I think competent, aggressive brokers more than earn their commissions.

F *inding the* **P** *erson* **W** *ho* **S** *uits* **Y** *ou*

I used to buy my suits off the rack. I'd go into a department store and look at the styles available in my size. I'd be bound to the styles and patterns in that store. Sometimes I'd like them and sometimes I wouldn't. Even if I went to the same store time and time again, the suits would fit me differently.

One day while walking in New York City, I saw a sign for a custom clothier. I walked in and looked around this impressive store. A gentleman asked if I needed help. He directed me to a table filled with samples of different materials. He said, "Take your time and look around." I was amazed at all the different types of materials they had for both suits and shirts. Before long, I had him come over and tell me the features of hundreds of different pieces of material.

He said, "Well, the main difference in these materials is the style, the quality, and the price." I thought, "Here it comes. He's ready to lay some heavy numbers on me." He started describing all the packages they had, including suit and shirt combinations. Then he suggested I go in the back to see how these suits were made so I had a better understanding of what I was purchasing. He told me about all the styles of suits available and the many measurements required for a custom-made suit. He told me that because a custom-made suit is designed specifically for the individual, it usually lasts three to four times longer than does the average suit.

After my education in suit-making, he told me the prices of the packages. I was absolutely floored. There were four levels of packages, and the third highest was the one I wanted. The fabrics looked great and the colors were perfect. I could buy three suits and six shirts for $2,000 in the exact style I wanted and in the fabrics that I liked best. That's less than what I pay in stores for off-the-rack suits.

He also said tailoring would be free for a year if I needed any adjustments resulting from changes in my weight. I must have been thinking about how great this deal was a little too long, because he chimed in and said, "If you'd like, I can charge you in ten payments of $200 each." I was sold.

He has not only "suited" me well but has also taught me that when it comes to yourself and your business, always get or hire the best. In the long run, they pay for themselves. They're great clothiers and can be found in my resource section at http://www.LargeRealEstate.com.

Contacting a Broker

Many real estate investors also have a broker's license so they can transact their own deals. (I say this is fine if you want to purchase properties in *only one area*, but if you're purchasing properties around the country, it's not worthwhile because of all the licensing requirements needed in each state.) A seller's broker will ask you up front: "Do you have a broker's license?" If you do, the seller's broker won't want to deal with you—unless, of course, you're willing to shelve your broker's license (that is, waive your share of the commission) for the deal. Brokers don't want to have to split their commissions with other brokers.

Another way to get in touch with commercial real estate brokers is to pick up the real estate section in a local newspaper. In most cities, the Sunday paper has a wealth of listings. Look for Investment Property, Commercial Property, or Income-producing Property—terms commonly used in the commercial real estate section.

Call the brokers listed with the properties you're interested in. Remember, you're searching for middle- to low-income properties. You can determine where middle- to low-income apartment buildings are located by phoning a real estate agency and asking. Easy enough.

H *e r e ' s   a*   T *i m e*   S *a v e r*

Position yourself for a good deal by calling brokers around 11:30 on Sunday nights when you know they won't be in their office. If you reach brokers during their workday, they typically ask lots of questions when all you want are property setup sheets. (Property setups are single sheets of paper listing facts about buildings that are for sale. Brokers send them to potential investors. If the preliminary numbers suit investors, they ask for more detailed numbers.) Leave a message like this: "Hi, I'm Greg Warr and I'm a commercial real estate investor. I'm calling about the ad you have in the Sunday paper (state which newspaper and give details about the ad). Please fax me a property setup sheet at the following number." Give your fax number. "If you need to reach me, I can be contacted at the following number between the hours of 9:00 AM to 6:00 PM. Thank you and have a good day."

Aggressive brokers will fax property setup sheets to you first thing Monday morning; nonaggressive ones will wait. Pay attention to which brokers give you the fastest response—that's good information to have when choosing the person you want to work with.

If you're still interested in properties after getting the setup sheets, call the brokers who are representing those properties. Warning: These brokers haven't had the pleasure of knowing you, so they may introduce you to any old deal they have. In fact, they may try selling you on their worst deal just because they want to dump that deal as fast as they can. In that case, how can you make the playing field more even? You ask for information, particularly information pertaining to the property you're calling about. Jot down the details they give you on your property setup sheet.

Next, analyze the property setup sheets (details in Chapter 7) and fax offers back within the next few hours. Responding quickly shows brokers you're a serious real estate investor. A serious investor means money in their pockets. Your speed also shows you're a professional who's worth their time.

If a property isn't great, you won't send back a great offer that's anywhere near the asking price. However, that indicates you want value. To make sure they realize that you want value, call them and say something like this: "I faxed an offer over to you early today. Did you get it? You know, this really isn't the ideal property for me. Do you have anything a little closer to what I'm looking for?" By making such a call, you've just told brokers you realize your offer was low, but if they want to keep you as a client, they'll find a good deal for you or you'll go to another broker who will.

Sometimes a good deal happens to fly into a broker's office while you're talking on the phone. Miraculously, he or she will share it with you. That's how it sometimes works!

Realize that the best deals *won't* be listed in the paper. Brokers know about them before they hit the papers and tell investors they know. That's why it's important to develop strong relationships with brokers in your area.

For more on good team members, go to http://www.Large RealEstate.com and click on team members.

BUYING IN EMPOWERMENT ZONES

If you've spotted any Empowerment Zones nearby, ask the brokers, "What product inventory do you have in these zones?" This is a way to find out if they're handling property that fits your investment criteria. (By the way, *product inventory* is a commercial real estate term for buildings in the area that are currently available.)

Give all brokers a list of your property guidelines and tell them to call you if they run across something that seems right for you. Your guidelines might include:

- Twenty-five-unit apartment buildings
- Two-bedroom apartments
- Low- to middle-income renters
- A specific area
- Section 8 eligibility

(Remember, Section 8 is a code that spells out the conditions for rent subsidies issued by HUD. See Chapter 2 for details.)

In an area where Section 8 monthly rent payments are $500 and the market rate is also $500 a month, building owners prefer to rent to individuals who can pay the full amount themselves. There's no incentive to do otherwise. But if there's a waiting list for apartments renting for $500, business owners can charge $600 a month and be guaranteed payment. Because HUD wants to be sure people aren't living on the street, it will be sure to pay.

A lot of investors want apartment buildings that are completely rented with Section 8 tenants because their rent payments are guaranteed. Sure, investors make good money, but most important, they provide homes for people who wouldn't have a place to live otherwise.

Another benefit of dealing with Section 8 tenants is that HUD has already screened them. You can further screen tenants using your own renting criteria. (Remember, though, sexual/racial discrimination is against the law.) Some of your criteria may be as follows: no pets, no convicts, or no welfare recipients.

I recommend you seriously consider investing in Section 8 commercial real estate. It means you're guaranteed the rent, sometimes being paid to do repairs, and sometimes getting tax breaks.

FINDING MANAGEMENT COMPANIES

While you're gathering brokers' names, also find out the names of property management companies. Interview selected property managers in the area and ask these questions:

- I'm looking to buy properties in this area. Do you have clients who are planning to sell some property or want to sell their own property?
- How long has your management company managed these target buildings?
- What repairs does the building need? (Owners don't always give the full story on repairs. I suggest you always ask, "If I buy this property, would you stay on as the management company?" If the managers hate working with these owners, they'll want out of it—a big clue. Generally, they'll tell you what's going right and what's going wrong.)
- If you are a licensed real estate broker, do you buy your own properties?
- Do you ever run across properties with the criteria I'm looking for?
- Do you know where there are other buildings I might invest in?

Ask if you can work through them if you find a property in the area you want to buy. They'll likely say yes because it can be a good piece of business for them. I suggest you deal with management companies that have a line into HUD and have at least one Section 8 property. That assures you that they understand rules and regulations required by HUD and the Section 8 code.

Getting a Building Up to Code

You want to get the Section 8 building you buy up to code, which means the building honors all the regulations spelled out in HUD's extensive code book. Just as important, you need to find a contractor who follows the code to a t. For example, if HUD requires three hinges on a kitchen cabinet and a contractor installs only two—to save money—the contractor has gone against code. Based on this, HUD inspectors could fail to approve the unit for its subsidized tenants. Management companies and contractors who've dealt with Section 8 know HUD guidelines and can expedite getting your property up to code.

For more on this, visit http://www.HUD.org and http://www.LargeReal Estate.com.

4

ANALYZING THE DEAL

I had to learn how to analyze deals on the fly. When I got into commercial real estate, I couldn't find any books about buying apartment buildings. I could only find books on buying single-family homes, in which the authors occasionally mentioned multiunits. But their idea of multiunits was 2 to 3 units whereas mine is 50 units or more.

In the beginning, I took the information from single-family units and applied it to multiunit apartment buildings—an archaic approach, but it got me started nonetheless. The numbers I analyzed weren't exact but close enough to get me in the door. I believe it's better to have a little information and move forward, regrouping later, than it is to sit around waiting for all the information you need. It doesn't mean I'm a cowboy when it comes to investing; it just means I'd rather be doing *something* than doing nothing.

When I applied information on structuring deals for single-family homes to an apartment building, the numbers I analyzed showed a hefty profit. I was nervous about those numbers, but I believed it could be a good deal even if my estimates were off by 50 percent. I decided to get an experienced investor interested in this deal who would put up approximately $1.5 million. (You might think $1.5 million seems like a big deal. In fact, it was a $4 million building in the 100-unit range. You might also think my advice contradicts what I do, because I suggested you start in a range between 10 and 25 units. But as people get older, they get wiser; and you're receiving the benefit of my wisdom and experience. Instead of trying to hit that home run right off the bat, I would have been better off hitting a few singles and doubles first to build momentum. You will too.)

I considered two avenues for finding a $1.5 million investor: I could approach a wealthy doctor, who might be an easy sell, or a seasoned real estate investor, who'd be tougher than a doctor but someone from whom I could learn a lot. I decided to go with the latter.

After making calls and placing ads in the paper, I got responses from a number of interested investors and set up a meeting with one investor named Charlie. I put as much information as I could into a brochure on the property. Then I added everything else I had, including my bio, to make my package as impressive as possible. (If all else fails, add weight!) All this impressed Charlie, who said, "As a seasoned real estate investor, I've never seen anything like this before." I felt on top of the world—but I was really standing on a sheet of ice.

As Charlie looked through the information, he first noticed a few mathematical errors. (That's why, to this day, I say, "Check your numbers at least three times.") Then he asked me a question I couldn't answer. This was one of only two times I can remember being at a loss for words! (You'll find out about the other time in a forthcoming book.) He asked: "What's the LTV?" (Just so you don't go into battle unprepared as I did, LTV stands for loan-to-value ratio.)

This critical datum refers to the amount you want to borrow as a percentage of the value of the property. For example, if a building is worth $1,000,000 and you want to borrow $800,000 to purchase it, then the LTV is 80 percent ($800,000 loan divided by $1,000,000 value equals 80 percent). I wish someone had taught me this before I confronted Charlie, because he's a gruff person with poor social skills, and that's being polite.

When he asked me about the LTV, I stared at him with my mouth open. I knew it was open, but I just couldn't close it. He looked at me again and raised his voice, asking the question louder, "What's the LTV?" At this point, I didn't know whether he was asking me for a name, or a number, or even a place. I couldn't bluff my way out of this one at all.

Have you ever experienced your body getting warm and things closing in around you? That's exactly how I felt sitting in that chair in his huge oak office. Charlie shouted again, "What's the LTV? 50, 60, 70?" At least he provided options for guessing, like a multiple-choice exam. I had a "vision" that the answer was 50, so I said, "50." In an even louder voice, he yelled, "50 percent?" I couldn't tell from his tone whether this number was good or bad, so I guessed again, saying, "Maybe 60?" If you're keeping track, I just jumped about half a million dollars in what I needed to borrow for this property.

Charlie shouted again, "60?" I still couldn't tell if this was right or wrong, so I blurted out, "It might be 70." And I still didn't understand whether I gave him a number or an address.

Charlie knew, though, that I'd just asked for another million-dollar leap on a property. He said, "You don't know what you're talking about. You don't even know what *the* LTV is, do you?" But he was wrong; I didn't even know what *an* LTV is!

Then he proclaimed, "I will never deal with you in real estate. You don't know what you're talking about." I felt about an inch tall. But I realized something. If he was a man of his word and really wouldn't deal with me again, that didn't mean I should just walk out without getting what I came for: knowledge.

So I said, "You're right. I don't know what LTV is." He nodded in agreement. Then I asked, "Well, what is it?" Purely through surprise at my frankness, I think, he told me the answer. Then I asked, "Why is it important?" He said, "Because it's easier to fund a lower LTV, since less money is required."

"Does that necessarily mean it's a good deal?" I asked, and the conversation continued like this for a while. I was learning from an extremely large real estate player in the world's greatest real estate playground, New York City.

After about an hour and a half, he realized what I was doing and gruffly exclaimed, "All right. That's it. School's out!" I walked away with my first big real estate lesson under my belt.

SKILL LEARNED THROUGH PRACTICE

How do you know if the building you're considering buying is a good investment? You know from your analysis; and that's why you analyze properties. The better you are at analyzing properties, the better real estate investor you'll become.

People aren't born with an innate ability to analyze properties. Rather, it's a skill that one develops through practice, practice, practice. If you're one of those individuals who says, "I'm not good with numbers," then fear not. Computers can handle the numbers. Still, you need to know the basics of analyzing a deal to better understand the piece of property you're about to buy.

As you learned in Chapter 2, you first call the commercial real estate broker to receive a property setup sheet. Once you have that, you have the preliminary numbers to put together a property analysis form. This form will tell you what the property is worth, what you can pay for it, and at the same time make a handsome profit. Isn't that what this is all about? Figure 4.1 is a sample setup sheet.

Reading the Setup Sheet

Remember that every property's setup sheet could be different; there is no standard format, but a comprehensive one, as shown in Figure 4.1, includes the elements described below.

FIGURE 4.1 *Sample Setup Sheet*

Warr Brokerage U.S.A.
123 Madison New York, NY 10002

6-unit all-brick walk-up

Location:	123 Elm St., Hometown, NY 12345
Size:	40 ft. × 60 ft.
Built:	1963
Description:	3-story walk-up, all brick
Layout:	2/5 2/4 2/3 Apartments 6 Rooms 24
Income:	Apartments $50,000
Estimated	R. E. Taxes $3,150
Expenses:	Water/Sewer $1,310
	Insurance $2,268
	Fuel (Oil #2) $985

Total Expenses. $7,713
Estimated Net Profit. $42,287

Asking:	$300,000 / owner will finance 80%
Remarks:	New roof, new boiler, and new windows

First, notice the address and contact information of the broker who sent you this information. Next comes a brief description of the property (such as "6-unit all-brick walk-up"). The next things listed are the address of the property and the size of the building (known as the "footprint" because when you look at it from the sky, the outline of the building looks like a footprint). The footprint indicates the length and the width of the building (40 ft. × 60 ft. in this example). Next is the year the building was constructed (1963).

The layout tells the number of units in the building and the number of rooms in each unit. The kitchen, living room, and all bedrooms are counted when calculating the number of rooms. A bathroom is typically not considered a room so it's not included. In this example, the layout is stated as 2/5, 2/4, 2/3.

Let's start with 2/5. The first number refers to the number of units in the building of this type (that is, there are two of these units). The next number, 5, states the number of rooms in each of these units (that is, the kitchen, living room, and three bedrooms). So in this example, there are two three-bedroom apartments (2/5), two two-bedroom apartments (2/4), and two one-bedroom apartments (2/3) in the building.

Now let's get to the core issue—the numbers representing dollars.

The first line indicates the income the building generates, or the total rent collected. (In commercial real estate, income numbers are recorded on a yearly basis unless otherwise noted.) If there is any additional income, such as income from a coin-operated laundry, pay telephones, or vending machines, that will be listed separately under "other income." Typically, that kind of income is stated separately to indicate how much money comes from rent and how much from other areas. Add them together to see how much you'd likely make from owning this building. In this example, the income from renting apartments is $50,000.

Realize that this is how much you'd collect under *ideal* situations—meaning all the tenants pay all the time on time. Unfortunately, this rarely occurs, so you're wise to make adjustments to the stated income. The first adjustment you'd make is a vacancy factor indicating how much of the time the units in this building are vacant. This property probably won't be fully occupied all of the time, so adjust for that now; eventually it would come out of your pocket. Even if you have a waiting list to rent in this building, when one tenant moves out, the apartment still needs to be painted and cleaned, which takes time. It's important to factor that in as well as any additional lag time between one tenant moving out and another moving in. That time between the two tenants means you're not receiving rent, and therefore you're losing money. The industry standard is a 5 percent vacancy factor, although it could be higher in different areas. Take time to ask a property management company in the area what that local vacancy factor is.

The next adjustment to make to the income is a collection factor. The collection factor refers to how much rent is not collected.

Get to Know Management Companies in the Area

A professional property management company can be a valuable part of your team, so become acquainted with those in your target areas. Seek companies that already manage properties in the area. Just drive around the area, find multiunit buildings that look well cared for, and ask who manages them. Call and inquire about hiring this company to manage your building if you decide to buy it.

Under perfect conditions, you'd collect 100 percent of the rent, but that's not reality. Take that into account before you buy this building. Again, the industry standard is 5 percent, but check with the management company to determine what the collection factor is in that specific area.

For this example, let's say that both the vacancy factor and collection factor are each 5 percent. Look at these calculations:

Income	$50,000
– Vacancy factor (5% of $50,000)	$ 2,500
– Collection factor (another 5% of $50,000)	$ 2,500
Effective gross income =	$45,000

After making your adjustments, you arrive at the effective gross income—the real-world number. Your effective gross income is the actual amount available to pay expenses, run the building, and make loan payments.

Listed next are the expenses for the building stated on a yearly basis. Often, not all of the expenses are included to allow the information to fit on one page. This is accomplished by taking all of the actual expenses from the building, adding them together, and dividing them into a few equal lines. That means when added together, they still equal the actual yearly expenses for the building. When noted this way, expenses are usually labeled "estimated expenses."

A second way to state expenses concisely is by omission. That means the sellers and their brokers aren't stating all the expenses associated with the property. Why? Because by keeping some of the expenses hidden, it makes the building appear more valuable, indicating that it doesn't cost that much to run. Don't worry. You'll find out what the actual numbers are after you make an offer on it, because you'll demand a detailed expense report in your contract. For the time being, these initial numbers suffice to help you determine how much the building is worth. They'll help you decide if it's even worth spending time to request a detailed expense report. When you subtract the expenses from the effective gross income, you get the net operating income, which is how much you'd make after paying the costs of the building.

Subtract the expenses from the income (the effective gross income).

Income	$50,000
– Vacancy factor (5% of $50,000)	$ 2,500
– Collection factor (another 5% of $50,000)	$ 2,500
Effective gross income =	$45,000
– Expenses	$ 7,713
NOI (net operating income) =	$37,287

Next, figure out how much this property is worth by using a shortcut—that is, multiplying the net operating income times 10, which is based on a scientific reason that's not necessary to explain here. This will give you a quick estimate of what the property is worth.

Property value (NOI × 10) = $37,287 × 10 = $372,870

In order to get a more exact estimate you will need to do three things:

1. Find out the exact interest rate you will be charged. For example, let's say that it is 7.5 percent (you know this because you get in touch with a mortgage lender and give them all of your information and the information on the property).

2. Add 2 to the interest rate. This gives you a cushion. So in this case, you are borrowing money at 7.5 percent (the number given to you by your mortgage lender) and want to make a return of 9.5 percent (7.5% plus your cushion of 2).

3. Divide the number from #2 above (9.5%) into your NOI to get the absolute maximum you can pay for a property (in this case, $37,287 ÷ .095 = $392,494.74; pretty close to the earlier estimate of $372,870).

This will give you a maximum purchase price with a small positive cash flow. If you need a larger cash flow, then just offer a lower price than $372,870. Just remember that my strategy dictates that you can't pay any more than this number (in this case, $372,870). Because I don't like doing all of these calculations by hand, I developed a program called REAPAC that will do all of this for you. You can learn more about it at http://www.Large RealEstate.com.

Congratulations! You have just figured out how much a property is worth based on its property setup sheet.

Make Your Offer

Next, write up an offer (see Chapter 7) and fax it to the broker. If the seller accepts your offer, request more detailed numbers on the building and run them the same way. Make sure the detailed numbers on the property match those on the property setup sheet. If the numbers aren't what you expected, you can either renegotiate the deal or decide not to buy the building by making a clear statement in the contract/offer. This statement is called an *addendum* or *stipulation* (also in Chapter 7).

If all goes well, you've just successfully analyzed a property and its value. However, if the owner rejects the offer right off the bat, then you can either drop the deal or renegotiate the contract. As a suggestion, continue negotiations only if the seller comes back with a counteroffer. If the response is "I decline the offer; send a new one," clearly state that you went to the effort to write a contract and would appreciate a response in kind. If the seller doesn't do that, stop the negotiations there.

In my experience, if sellers aren't willing to write a counteroffer, then they're just fishing around to see how high they can get you to increase your price without having to make a counteroffer. I fell for that trap once but won't fall for it again.

A NUMBERS GAME

No matter how much you work at it and how creative you get, real estate investing is based on the law of large numbers. That means you need to analyze a lot of properties and make a lot of offers.

Here's my approach. I don't focus on the asking price; I look at it only after I analyze the deal to see if my offer price and the asking price are close together. And the degree of separation determines the amount of time and energy I invest. For example, if my analysis comes up with $1.25 million and the seller is asking $3.5 million, this huge difference doesn't stop me from putting in an offer. It simply determines how much emphasis and effort I put into the deal. So if the numbers are far apart, I quickly put together an offer and send it out. If they're close, I put more creativity into the deal.

5

GATHERING MORE DETAILS

After you do the initial analysis on a property, it's time to gather more detailed information so you can make an informed decision about buying it. Is it a good buy or not?

Realize that sellers tend to withhold information about the building to make the deal look better. They might state income on the high side and expenses on the low side so the property appears to be more profitable than it is. Your job is to obtain more information and, once you have it, determine how it will affect the deal. If the numbers shift significantly from your first analysis to your final analysis (and they do 90 percent of the time), you might decide to walk away from this opportunity.

Start by gathering additional information through a management company (either one currently in place or one in the area that manages buildings comparable to the one you're analyzing). The professionals there know what it costs to manage and maintain this kind of building in this particular area. Ask about maintenance costs, taxes, and insurance. Hiring a good management company is integral to your success in running a building profitably, so carefully check out companies in the area.

If the company's representatives aren't responsive when you call to request information, you'll already know a lot about how the company runs its business. If they take a long time to return your calls, they'll still probably take a long time to return your calls after you buy the building. Beware!

Think of your team members as your employees. You are their manager; the management company is an integral part of your team. The management company works with you in return for commissions ranging from 5 to 10 percent. Pay particular attention to the types of properties that companies manage, and hire one that specializes in the type of property you own. Make sure this company has a long, reputable track record.

Conducting the Orchestra

Remember, you're the team leader. Like a conductor of an orchestra, you need broad-based knowledge of a lot of information. What does the conductor do? He or she directs the tempo, creates emphasis, and times the cutoffs. The conductor needs to understand the mechanics of the music, not how to play every instrument.

Your role is similarly broad-based as you conduct the activities of your specialized team members. You should be able to rely on their knowledge without having to be an expert yourself. Most new real estate investors do the opposite—they're detail oriented but hire generalists to work for them. This is a mistake you don't want to make.

Some management companies say they can manage any type of building. That isn't good enough. Because you want each team member to be specialized, your management company should specifically deal with residential commercial property of five units or more, because that's the type of property you're looking for.

BASE INFORMATION GATHERING ON YOUR CRITERIA

Now you're gathering additional information on your property based on the following criteria: type of property, size of property (physical), and number of units. These three criteria provide you with most of the information you need. You already have the numbers; now you're polishing the analyses with specific information.

You'll find two types of buildings that have five or more units: high-rise buildings or town houses. High-rises are more common in cities where land is tight; town houses are prevalent where there is more land to build on.

Here's what the difference means in maintenance. A high-rise building will be self-contained—all the hallways are inside the building and no balconies are outside; town houses, on the other hand, have some outside exposure. Where high-rises have only one roof, town houses, depending on the number of units, have from 5 to 20 roofs. High-rises have one boiler; town houses from six to eight. (Boilers are a high-cost maintenance item.) Be sure your management company understands the difference between managing high-rises and managing town houses.

Different Challenges

It may seem as though I'm favoring high-rises, but town houses have their advantages. Because they have more land with more greenery, they're more pleasing to the eye. They remind people of single-family homes, and that means curb appeal to attract better tenants.

As you start purchasing buildings that have more units, your challenges change. By increasing the building size, you can drastically increase, percentagewise, the number of people per building. For example, a 20-unit building could accommodate 40 people, whereas a 100-unit building could accommodate 200 people, which is a huge increase in the wear and tear on your building.

Here's a small example of a maintenance issue for large buildings. Usually, people enter and exit through one main entry, so the larger building's front door gets more use than a smaller building's. That also means the main hallway carpet wears out more quickly. A good management company suggests that this main hall floor should be tiled, not carpeted. So it's imperative that you hire the right management company to help you keep costs down.

When analyzing buildings, you always benefit from gathering lots of information. You generally go through the same cycle to get it: obtain general preliminary information, review it, and gather more detailed information. After you've owned two or three buildings with 10 to 25 units each, you'll move up to 50 units, then 100. At first, you'll need a management company that knows how to run the smaller apartment buildings. As you progress in unit size, you'll likely need a new management company. Hire for the expertise you need.

Offices Everywhere

As my portfolio of real estate has increased, so has my scope of investing. Whereas I used to invest in only one area (New York City), I now invest throughout the country. To stress the importance of information, I'll use the example of my office space.

As I started to buy properties across the states, I needed to have instant access to information about potential properties. Having my office in only one area of the country was slowing me down, so I started renting office space through a company (these companies are referred to as satellite office space companies), which provided offices throughout the country. I still have an office in New York but can also use space from this company in any city in which I have property—all for about the same price. With the Internet, when I step into an office in a new city, it's as though I'm still in my own headquarters.

Why did I tell you this? Because information is extremely important. Set yourself up to have as much information as possible rather than investing with your eyes closed. My motto is "Show me the info!"

For more on setting up your office or getting office space, click on *office space* at http://www.LargeRealEstate.com.

RESEARCH THE INCOME SIDE OF THE EQUATION

Income is one of the most important factors to consider when buying real estate. Do your research through the management company to find out various rent amounts in the area. What are the top rents, lowest rents, and average rents? What do renters expect for the money they pay? If a seller says you can get $500 a month for units currently renting at $350 a month, be cautious. The seller might claim he's softhearted and just didn't want to raise the rent on long-term residents. Chances are greater that he hasn't kept the building up and therefore *can't* demand higher rents. If that's true and you expect to collect $500 a month per unit, you'll likely have to make significant repairs, starting with increasing the building's curb appeal to attract new tenants who'll pay higher rents. You might also have to spruce up the façade, replace the carpets, paint the hallways, and even rehab the apartments. (Be sure to include costs to do all of this in your expense totals when doing your analysis.)

To determine your ideal market rents, start by conducting market research—talking to brokers, other investors, and management companies. Remember, this research is largely opinion based, so be sure to seek people experienced in these areas. And remember, no opinion is carved in stone. Gather "comps" based on buildings of the same age, condition, and size. Also ask owners of similar properties nearby what they charge for rents. Beware asking the owner of the property you want to buy, as you

---

R e a c h   a   **H** i g h e r   **L** e v e l   o f   **C** o m p e t i t i o n

After college, I trained for the Iron Man competition. I had trained well for running, but I needed to improve my swimming, so I worked with a swim coach at my YMCA. After working with me for a while, my coach told me he'd taken me as far as he could. He was a gruff, tough coach like one in the movies, and his announcement shocked me. I'd assumed he'd be tough enough to take me all the way. But he knew how high my goal was—to excel in the Iron Man competition—and he knew his limitations. So he suggested I join Columbia University's swim team, which I did. In retrospect, I was grateful that he brought me up to a certain level and then sent me off to reach the next.

Similarly, as you progress in this business, you'll need new and better coaches and team members. You'll outgrow some and need to move on. In particular, the management company you started with in your real estate investing business probably won't be able to serve you all the way through your career, so prepare for that.

---

might get an inflated number to make the deal look more attractive. A wise man once told me: "What's true is only true for you." That means the burden of proving the truth of other's statements rests on your shoulders.

I suggest taking the same advice that my mentor gave me: "Your first goal in buying property is to produce an income." By comparison, a single-family house is designed for a family to live in, not to produce income. Homeowners benefit by having a place to live where they can raise a healthy, happy family. If the house makes money for them, well then, that's a bonus. By living in the house for many years, they've realized its main benefit.

On the other hand, the purpose of an income-producing single-family house is different. Your tenants must be happy so they'll stay in your home and keep paying rent. However, your *main* purpose for their living there is not to make them happy but to produce income for yourself. (Happy tenants equal income.) Then you can take that money and buy a second property and a third and a fourth.

Assess Market Rents through Ads

In addition to conducting opinion-laden market studies to determine market rents, it's wise to place Apartment for Rent ads in the local newspaper. List the number of bedrooms the apartments in your target building has, the part of town it's in, and *your guess* at the market rent. Don't do this on a whim, though. You fully intend to buy the property and get new tenants, so it's prudent to *advertise before you buy*. You'll even have the right to show the property (see Chapter 7 for details on how to set that up).

Let's say you guess the rent will be $750 a month for a one-bedroom apartment. You have these options: List $750 as rent and track the number of calls you get; or tell callers you're in the process of buying the building, are taking applications, and will get in touch with them when vacancies open up. Let's say your ad generates 10 calls. Is that good? You don't know if that's a lot of calls—yet.

Next, run an ad listing the rent at $700 a month; this ad generates 50 calls. Then you run an ad at $850 a month and get no calls. When you lower the rent to $825, you get a handful of calls; and at a rental rate of $800 a month, you get 5 calls. This tells you that the market rents are between $700 and $750. Stay in touch with those callers, because you've used this process not only to determine market rent rates, but also to assemble a database of potential renters. Use this strategy for each type of unit you have available for rent: studio, two-bedroom, and so on.

You also can look in local magazines that list current rent for apartments. They come at a major cost, though: free. You usually can find them in boxes at street corners and also in the waiting areas of restaurants like Denny's. So grab a bite to eat and do some market research. Also, for more on market rents look on the Internet in search engines to get rentals in the area in which you are looking to buy.

Review Maintenance History

Gather as much information about the building's maintenance history as possible by consulting the property setup sheet and asking the real estate broker a lot of questions. (I'd suggest getting a detailed maintenance list for the property, but each maintenance situation is specific to the building and its previous owners, so the list won't give you much meaningful information.)

Maintenance refers to the hourly, daily, monthly, and yearly upkeep of the building. For instance, you need to paint walls and clean carpets once a year, maintain the boiler quarterly, mow the lawns weekly, and clean up trash daily (especially on Mondays because people party over the weekends and let the trash pile up). You want the property to look especially nice on Monday evenings, because prospective tenants usually look through ads in the Sunday newspaper and then come after work at the beginning of the week to look at your property.

K*eeping* U*p* A*ppearances*

By observing the maintenance standards of other properties in the area, you can easily narrow your search for a management company. How? Just drive around the area, and if you see properties that are kept up and are more appealing than others, find out who's managing them. Be sure to look on Sundays and Mondays. On Sundays, notice how dirty the weekend activities made the property. Then, on Mondays, observe how well the management company cleaned it up.

Inspect the building to find out what needs to be upgraded (furnaces, boilers, electrical boxes, windows, roofs, and so on). Is the foundation or brickwork solid or does either need a lot of repair? Look at the landscaping and sidewalks in front of the building. Find out who takes care of sidewalks—the building owners or the city. Thoroughly estimate what repairs and maintenance items will be crucial for you to take care of if you own this property.

To learn more about fix–ups, go to one of these giant home improvement stores and start looking at the prices of materials. If you know what the materials cost you'll have a good idea of what you will be charged. Some stores will even give you books and CDs of their products, costs, and estimated work time to accomplish these. My Web site, http://www.LargeRealEstate.com, also will give you some estimates; just click on *rehabs* or *team members*.

Swimming Pools On-site

Most middle- to low-income properties don't have swimming pools on-site, and that's the way you'd prefer it because pools increase insurance and maintenance costs. Covering costs for swimming pools come from tenants' rents, so I'd prefer tenants didn't have to pay extra for something they rarely use. The important thing for them is a safe, secure, and clean environment rather than amenities. Luxury properties often have pools along with doormen, awnings, and such services as laundry, but those aren't the kinds of buildings you want to buy as your goal is to make a good profit.

EXAMINE MAINTENANCE COSTS

Before you buy the building, make sure you know what it will cost to maintain on a daily basis. Keep in mind that having a messy building ultimately costs you in curb appeal. People won't want to live there.

The preliminary maintenance numbers only provide a snapshot of costs. It's important to ask if the costs will be consistent month after month. For example, in Buffalo, New York, you pay a lot for snow removal in winter but nothing in the summer months. During hurricane season in Florida, you have to anticipate higher costs for cleanup and power outages.

Paint the Best Picture Possible

Know that sellers paint the best picture possible; for example, they may show you numbers on a low-expense month but not a high-expense month. Therefore, insist on reviewing two whole years of numbers. Ask a lot of questions, particularly relating to seasonal costs. If you didn't see a line item for snow removal for that building in Buffalo, New York, then the seller may be trying to "snow you." Omissions like that also reveal the mentality of sellers. Take that information to heart and ask yourself, "What else are they hiding?"

Often the management company takes care of cleaning, painting, and changing locks, then hires a contractor to do major repairs (after getting at least three estimates). Always outline which repairs the company is responsible for up to a certain dollar amount. For example, have the management company handle any maintenance or repair costs that run less than $200.

When you buy a property, assign maintenance issues on one of three levels of importance:

1. Things that *have to* be done
2. Things that *should be* done
3. Those things that would be *nice to have* done

Let's say the boiler isn't running, and the backup boiler is run down—this is a "has to be done" item. Window caulking is a "should be done" item, as it cuts down on heating and cooling costs. A "nice to be done" item might be cleaning the soot from the front of the building or replacing frayed awnings. It raises the property value to have a clean, nice-looking building, but this isn't necessary for running the building.

HIRING INSPECTORS

Before finalizing your purchase, hire three (always do things in threes) building inspectors to go into the property and tell you what it looks like in detail. Select only licensed, independent building inspectors. You might even hire an inspector who owns a construction company and brings that knowledge into the inspection process. Now, you may argue that contractors who are inspectors have ulterior motives. Get around that objection by making sure they know you're getting three separate inspections. They then get the message that, if they want the job making repairs, their bids will have to be competitive.

Be Prepared for Costly Repairs

One of the biggest mistakes new investors make is not being prepared for unexpected and costly building repairs. The three biggest expenses in a building are the boiler, roof, and windows. If the boiler goes out at 2:00 AM on a cold morning, you'll be taken to the cleaners by the first repair service that can get there to fix it. This can run up to $60,000 or more! If you've done your homework, you'd have a qualified contact to call before that happens.

You'll have to pay for the inspection, which ranges from $500 to $1,000 for a 20-unit building. (Fees vary from place to place.) Have the inspectors include a detailed list of repairs, costs, and time needed to complete the repairs. Also ask for photographs with their lists as well as a breakdown of material and labor costs.

CALCULATE FINANCING COSTS

At this point, you need in-depth calculations of your financing costs. Initially, it's easy to put a round figure like 6 percent or 7 percent on paper to estimate long-term mortgage or debt service. Get in touch with lenders you want to work with. Find out what interest percentage they'd charge you. (You'll get a lower interest rate if you have a good track record and credit score. See Chapter 1.) Find out, to the fraction of a point, exactly what you'd have to pay. Remember, the larger the building you buy, the greater the difference each fraction of a percentage point makes.

When you're financing your purchase, be aware of what's happening with the economy. For example, when interest rates are low, banks lend money to lots of buyers because they need the high volume of loans to compensate for low interest rates. In times like that, asking prices for buildings are often inflated. Why? Because mortgage money is easily available. However, when interest rates are high, buyers are more finicky about their purchases because they can't afford to buy as many properties and take as many risks as when money is cheap, that is, interest rates are low.

Say you're given a monthly payment structure to pay off your loan. Now you have a choice: You can take your cash flow and buy more property, or you can use it to pay down the principal. If you pay down the principal, the result is similar to lowering your interest rate because you're lowering the total dollar amount owed.

W_hen to_ **P**_ay_ **D**_own_ **D**_ebt_

I'll share a secret I learned from wealthy investors. A simple process for deciding when to pay down debt is called "9.0 to 9.1." This is how it works. Money is considered cheap when it's borrowed at 9.0 percent interest or less. When interest rates are low and money is cheap, you want to borrow as much as possible and buy as much property as you can. But when money is expensive—9.1 percent or more—you want to artificially lower interest rates by paying down the principal. That way, you pay down the overall amount of debt service—in effect, decreasing your interest rate.

GETTING DETAILS FROM SELLERS

To get to the point of being able to close on a property, you looked at general information. Once the deal has been accepted as stipulated in the contract, then demand to review detailed expense reports. You can get them in one of three forms:

1. Three years of tax returns
2. Audited financial statements
3. Independent management company reports

Tax returns. You want to see what the sellers have reported to the IRS about operating the building. You can usually rely on those figures. (Generally, sellers are more honest on tax returns than they are with investors.) If they refuse to show you their tax returns, move on. They're hiding something.

Audited financial statements. If sellers don't want to show you tax returns because their returns will reveal their other sources of income, audited financial statements can work just as well.

Have an independent auditor go through the sellers' tax forms, extracting all information pertaining to the building.

Independent management company reports. By independent, I mean a company that's not connected to the building you want to buy or to the owners themselves. An independent management company is obligated as a business to show you the appropriate records. It has nothing to gain by showing you faulty information.

G *et* F *ull* C *ooperation*

It's a good idea to make sure that you have the independent management company's *full* cooperation. How do you do this? Ask: "If I decide to buy this property, would you consider staying on as the management company?" Of course, this doesn't obligate you to use that company, but if things work out well, you might. The company understands that if it manages your building and you find out it gave you misinformation, you'd fire the company. You might even take it to court.

Should the management report be audited? Not necessarily. The management company, acting as an independent contractor, is legally liable for any misinformation it gives potential buyers.

Sometimes owners manage their own properties, keeping all the records for the property themselves. These people have objectives other than just managing the property, so it's in their best interest to make the books reflect profits as high as possible in order to obtain the best purchase price for the property. In that case, you *have* to take sellers' word about some issues about the property, but you *don't* have to take their word about income and expense records. That's why you don't want managing owners' records; you want an independent's records! The answer is to go back to getting tax returns or financial statements. In business, this is called "checks and balances."

Remember, it can be a costly decision to purchase property without first looking at three years of tax returns, audited financial statements, or independent management company reports. Don't make any exceptions!

STRESSING NET OPERATING INCOME

If you subtract the expenses (money going out) from the income (money coming in), you have the net operating income (NOI) for a property (see Chapter 4). The NOI dictates what the property is worth. If your analysis shows high income and low expenses, your NOI is high—but double-check your information. (Sellers naturally try to make income numbers look big and expense numbers look small so the NOI looks good on paper. In the financial markets, that's called *paper profit*.)

Once you've carefully calculated the NOI, you'll have a better understanding of the costs and value of the building. The lesson is this: Don't take the original analysis numbers at face value. If your second analysis raises too many red flags, there's no point moving forward. You want to be efficient and maximize your time, so your objective for an additional analysis is to answer this question: Do you want to move forward with the deal?

In your analysis, the NOI is your most important number. Be absolutely sure about each factor that goes into calculating the NOI because all judgments are made from this number: what the value is, what the return is, whether the lender is willing to lend, and whether the investor is willing to invest. In short, the NOI tells you the viability of the property as an investment. If you don't get these numbers right, you can forget about getting money from lenders and investors, plus you jeopardize providing renters with a place to live and risk going into foreclosure.

The NOI is the subfactor of everything else you've done up to this point. That's why I say if you can't get detailed reports from the seller, you can't move forward with the deal. You have to move on—this is your livelihood after all.

Adjusting Property Taxes

When a building is sold, the property taxes on that building often increase. The city almost automatically takes this opportunity to assess more taxes, which increases your expenses, decreases your NOI, and decreases the property's value. To find out what the new tax amount will be, go to the courthouse and talk with a tax assessor.

A common mistake investors make is trying to get the tax rate lowered. If a new property owner waltzes into the tax assessor's office and asks for the tax rate on the building to be lowered, the tax assessor will likely say no. What went wrong here? The new owner asked the wrong question. Instead, the question should be: "*When* do you lower taxes?"

You see, tax assessors typically lower taxes only one day a year; they have other things to deal with the rest of the time. If you walk in and ask the assessor to lower your taxes on the wrong day, you're out of luck. That's why you should also ask: "What information do you need to review the taxes on the building?" Then get the information together and be prepared for "the" day.

If the assessor does indeed lower the taxes on the building, your next question should be: "Can you make that retroactive?" (You're wise to gain rapport with the assessor before you ask this.) Here are the three questions again: When do you lower taxes? What information do you need before reviewing the taxes? Can you make that change retroactive? Doing that will increase your probability of saving money on taxes, so don't miss this opportunity.

6

USING CREATIVE FINANCING

Your goal is to create maximum leverage to make the most of your buying dollar. Creative financing can help you accomplish this. I'm not talking about using tricks or confusing sellers with fancy lingo, but rather increasing your buying dollar in a way that benefits both you *and* the seller. Creative financing simply makes sure deals result in wins for both sellers and buyers—win-win deals. If they're not win-win, they're flawed and unacceptable deals, which you clearly don't want.

Remember, a win-win deal doesn't necessarily mean the sellers will agree to your terms; instead, it means offering them the maximum possible and still having attractive and profitable deals left for yourself. This way, both parties walk away happy. That's a win-win situation.

In Chapters 4 and 5, you learned how to determine what a property is worth (that is, the most you can pay for a property and still make money). Using that information—the property's worth or maximum dollar figure—you have to figure out how to convince the sellers to accept that dollar figure (or less) and create a win-win situation. This is where *creative financing* strategies through conventional and/or private funding come in.

Later in this chapter, I will also show you an interesting creative strategy you can use with a corporation instead of just creative financing with the building.

CONVENTIONAL FINANCING

Conventional financing is a common method buyers use to purchase properties. You can obtain the financing through working with a bank or private financing (financing that comes from a private source such as a private corporation) or independent lenders. You'll typically use conventional financing to cover the majority of your purchase price.

First, find out if there's already conventional financing in place on the property. If so, ask the seller if you could take over (assume) this financing, provided the original conventional financing source allows it. If you're not allowed to assume the financing, or there's no financing to assume anyway, then your number-one priority is finding conventional financing. Your best bet is to go to a private financing source because large institutions like a major bank require steep standards of qualification before they will lend the funds.

PRIVATE FINANCING

How can you find private sources? Look for listings in your local newspaper under the category Real Estate: Money to Lend. Within that category, look for phrases like "private money to lend," "investor with money to lend," or "hard moneylender." When you call lenders from these ads, ask about their terms and determine what types of properties they lend money on. You can request this information before or after you've found a property. However, I think it's best to call *before* you find property, so you'll know what lenders' criteria are before you even start analyzing ones that interest you. Doing this gives you a sense of whether you can even borrow enough to buy the property you're analyzing.

Another way to locate private financing sources is to contact commercial real estate brokers, also listed in your newspaper's real estate section. You can also ask for referral from any management companies you've developed relationships with.

Next, contact the brokers and ask, "What programs do you have for purchasing commercial real estate?" This question ferrets out the types of properties they are looking for and their debt service terms. Once you know these criteria, you're armed with the ability to quickly structure a deal. Why? Because you have the appropriate potential lenders lined up. Creative lenders are out there. I hear a lot of the time "That can't be done" only to ask the same person "How many people did you talk to?" The common response is "One." And that one time it's usually a relative who knows nothing about real estate. Creative lenders are out there with lots of money, and even if they weren't, most of the real estate you see today would be around. Successful real estate investors not only find "creative money," they also demand that it's available!

For more on commercial lending, click on *lending* at http://www.LargeRealEstate.com and also network with the people you talk to in real estate, such as real estate brokers. Networking is always a good way to learn, once you know the strategies and what can be done.

Terminology to Know

In commercial property, the total amount of money you borrow is called debt service; in residential property it's called a mortgage. In effect, mortgage and debt service are the same thing except that the term *debt service* is applied to commercial real estate.

Calculating Loan to Value

In Chapter 4, you read my story about Charlie, who introduced me to a concept called *loan to value* (LTV). Remember, LTV is the ratio between the amount of money you're borrowing and the value of the property.

For example, let's say a property is worth $1 million and you want to borrow $800,000 to purchase that property. You take the amount you want to borrow (which is $800,000 in this case) and divide it by the value of the property (the most you can pay for a property—the maximum dollar figure—and still make money, which is $1 million). You end up with .8 or 80 percent LTV. Therefore, you're financing 80 percent of the value of the property.

$$\text{Loan amount} \div \text{Property value} = \text{LTV}$$
$$\$800,000 \div \$1,000,000 = .8\ (80\%)$$

Lenders will tell you the LTV they're most comfortable with for a particular property. Once you know this, you can calculate how much you have left to finance. In this example, that means you have $200,000 more to finance to complete the deal.

$$\text{Purchase price} - \text{LTV} = \text{Amount left to finance}$$
$$\$1,000,000 - \$800,000\ (80\%) = \$200,000$$

Two Ways to Finance the Remainder

How can you creatively finance the remaining money to make this deal happen? Through seller financing and/or through investor financing. Let's look at both options.

Seller financing. Ask the sellers if they would accept the remaining $200,000 in the form of a note (called seller financing). Request that they hold that $200,000 note at, or lower than, the market interest rate. If market rates are 6 percent, for example, you want the sellers to hold $200,000 at 6 percent for as long as possible. (In most real estate transactions, that's 30 years with monthly payments of $1,200. Find this number by using a real estate calculator or software program.) Start your negotiations here. If that amount isn't acceptable to the sellers, either raise the interest rate or change the span of time for making payments. Which one would you adjust first? Ask the sellers. Do they want more money, or do they want the loan paid off sooner rather than later?

Whatever adjustment you come up with, put it into your analysis to make sure that the building will generate enough income to cover payments on this loan. Subtract the "total" monthly payment (conventional financing plus seller financing) from the NOI to come up with the cash flow number.

Net operating income – Total debt service = Cash flow

To summarize, ask the sellers to carry the balance left after your conventional financing. Negotiate the terms. Tell your lenders that you intend to have the seller carry a note. It's your job as a professional real estate investor to line up lenders with whom you can make special arrangements.

Investor financing. If you can't convince the sellers to carry the full balance, ask what part of the balance they *will* carry. Negotiate the terms. Then find an investor to finance the rest.

Again, the analysis is this:

Net operating income (NOI) – total debt service = cash flow

So here's how it can work: You *ask* the sellers to hold $200,000 as a note (seller financing). They agree to hold $100,000 at 6 percent interest for 30 years. Next, you ask a real estate investor to finance the remaining $100,000 at 6 percent interest for 30 years

---

Finding **I**nvestor **F**inancing

I've found the best way to find an investor is to place an ad in the newspaper. Offer real estate investors a good return on their investment—an amount dictated by the value of the property. Remember, you can't afford to pay the investor more than you make from the building (cash flow). The most you can pay for the property is what you have as net operating income. If you pay any more than that, you lose money. Just work backward from your NOI.

(or a similar arrangement that still allows you to make a profit). Keep this in mind: If there's no financing on the property to begin with, *you can ask the sellers to hold 100 percent of the purchase price* of the building. There's nothing that says you can't ask them to finance the whole purchase.

All creative financing stems from variations of this basic format. Learn to use it well.

Be **E**ven **M**ore **C**reative

Here's an example of getting even more creative with your financing. (Remember, this is just one of the thousands of variations on this basic format.) Say you ask the sellers to hold $200,000, but they agree to hold only $100,000. You can sweeten the pot by saying, "If you hold *$150,000,* I'll pay 6 percent for the first three years, 7 percent for the next three years, and 8 percent for the term of the loan." If they jump at this opportunity, then you'll only need to borrow $50,000 from a real estate investor instead of $100,000.

THE POWER OF COMPOUNDING INTEREST

When you calculate your offers, understand the power of compounding interest inherent in borrowing funds. Compounding interest—what Albert Einstein called man's greatest invention—can work for you or it can work against you. That is, when you're *paying* compounding interest, it's working *against* you and when you're *earning* compounding interest, it's working *for* you.

I want you to realize how dramatic compounding interest can be. For example, if I hire you for 30 days and teach you everything I know, I can pay you two ways: $1,000 a day for a total of $30,000, or one cent a day and double it for 30 days. Which way would you prefer?

First, as always in real estate, do the math. The following shows you what happens with the compounding interest option:

Day 1—1 cent
Day 2—2 cents
Day 3—4 cents
Day 4—8 cents
Day 5—16 cents
Day 6—32 cents
Day 7—64 cents
Day 8—1 dollar and 28 cents

By Day 16, you still won't be making a lot of money ($327.28). But what happens by Day 30? Keep doing the math and find out. At the end of Day 30, you'll have $10,737,418.24. (Unfortunately, I've already filled that position—sorry.) But the question remains, "Do you want to *pay* compounding interest or *earn* compounding interest?"

Developing My Own System

When I started in real estate, I had to learn creative financing the hard way and the lessons were painful. I knew from talking to top investors that to make good deals, I'd have to write a lot more offers than experienced investors did. Consistently putting out offers over and over again helped me feel comfortable with the numbers. That way, if there was a change in the interest rate or a change in the expense, I'd know how to make adjustments quickly and easily. From the lessons I've learned and the confidence I've acquired, I developed the system I'm sharing with you. One of the main things I'm teaching you in this book is to increase your net worth. In real estate and specifically business, net worth is everything. If you don't know what your net worth is, don't know how to figure it, or want to see if you are on the right track with building your net worth (in addition to what I'm teaching you), then visit http://www.FindYourNetWorth.com.

Even if you start working your business for only a half hour a day, I suggest you still put out offers and continue to build momentum. Be consistent, practice discipline, and follow the system you're learning in this book.

CREATIVE CORPORATE FINANCING

Money can be made in many ways. In this strategy, I quickly want to tell you about a way to not only save it but also to get a tax write-off because of it.

One tax code states that if your business can use a truck then you can write it off. In real estate, would a truck come in handy?

Now the tax code states that if you purchase a 6,000-pound truck or more, you can accelerate the depreciation (on http://www.LargeRealEstate.com we'll keep an updated list of these vehicles). Depreciation means that you can use this as a tax deduction.

Here's how it works. Buy one of these 6,000-pound trucks or more to help in your real estate business. Some of these trucks are pretty fancy. The government says that you can accelerate the depreciation on that vehicle and write off up to $25,000 immediately.

To show you the importance of moving quickly and decisively in real estate and real estate–related matters, when I wrote this chapter the tax deduction was $100,000. Two days later, the IRS said it was lowering the deduction to $25,000. It may not affect us as real estate investors, but the main thing I wanted to show is that in real estate (and life) you want to move quickly because you never know when situations may change.

This is the exact reason I put together the reference site http://www.LargeRealEstate.com, to report about changes that will be on the cutting edge. On the site I'll explain why this particular change by the IRS affects us.

Now most of the trucks that you might buy would be in the $50,000–$60,000 range, which would be a nice immediate deduction, or what the federal government calls accelerated depreciation.

Even better, let's say you lease this vehicle. You make a lease payment of about $600 or $1,000 and get an immediate tax advantage of up to $25,000; $600 for $25,000, now that's smart.

It means you can start your real estate business with a corporation, get a new truck, and immediately have up to a $25,000 tax advantage to apply to your first real estate deal.

One caveat: I suggest that you talk with a professional such as an attorney or CPA before you apply any strategy like this.

7

STRUCTURING THE OFFER AND NEGOTIATING

How would you like someone to do your negotiating for you—What if this negotiator also had a legal background and understood how to get you out of any deal with just one sentence?

What if this negotiator had the knowledge of hundreds of successful investors before you?

This ideal negotiator does exist—in the form of a legal offer document that's called "an investor's purchase and sale contract and addenda." Most people are under the false assumption that a contract is only used for putting on paper what two parties have already agreed on. That's correct if that's how the two parties *decide* to use a contract. But I've been taught that a contract is your frontline form of negotiation. If you keep that in mind, this chapter will not only make sense to you but will also make millions for you.

CONTRACTS

You've analyzed the deal and understand creative financing with its various strategies. Now let's look at how to put that groundwork into an offer document or contract.

I am not an attorney or accountant, and I don't provide legal advice, but I'm willing to share the contract I use as a guide for creating your own. Be sure to have an attorney check it out for you. (You'll find my sample contract in this chapter and you can also get a copy electronically from my Web site at http://www .LargeRealEstate.com under Resources.)

Before visiting your attorney, obtain a state contract form that's specific to the state in which you do business. You can generally buy one from an office supply store, from brokers, or online.

When you visit your attorney, say, "I'm using this basic contract that came from Greg Warr as a boilerplate. Then I want to include the important points from the state contract. Can you help me do this?" Have your attorney point out the important points and then type them into your contract. If you're able to download the state contract online, you simply have to cut and paste changes into it on your computer. In fact, I recommend putting your contract on your computer to use as a boilerplate contract. That way, you can easily fill in the specifics each time you make an offer.

FIGURE 7.1 *Contract for Sale and Purchase*

Parties: _____ , as "Seller"

of _____ (Phone)

and _____ , as "Buyer"

of _____ (Phone)

hereby agree that the seller shall sell and the buyer shall buy the following property upon the following terms and conditions WHICH INCLUDE the Standards For Real Estate Transactions on the reverse hereof or attached hereto, hereinafter referred to as "Standard(s)."

I. DESCRIPTION:

    (a) Legal Description of real estate ("Property") located in _____ County, to be supplied by seller within 10 days after acceptance

    (b) Street address, if any, of the Property being conveyed is _____

    (c) Personal property included: _____

    _____

II. PURCHASE PRICE: $_____

    Payment:

    (a) Deposit(s) to be held in escrow by closing agent, in the amount of $_____

    (b) Subject to loans in favor of bearing interest at _____ % per annum and payable as to principal and interest _____ per month, having an approximate present principal balance of $_____

    (c) Purchase money note bearing interest at _____ % on terms set forth herein below, in the principal amount of $_____

    Other $_____

    (d) Balance to close, subject to adjustments and prorations exactly. $_____

    TOTAL $_____

III. FINANCING: If the purchase price or any part thereof is to be financed by a third party loan, this Contract for Sale and Purchase ("Contract") is conditioned upon the Buyer obtaining a firm commitment for said loan within sixty (60) days from the date hereof, at an interest not to exceed _____ %; term of _____ years; and in the principal amount of _____. Buyer agrees to make application for, and to use reasonable diligence to obtain, said loan. Should Buyer fail to obtain same or waive Buyer's rights hereunder within said time, either party may cancel contract.

IV. TITLE EVIDENCE: Within thirty (30) days from date of Contract, Seller shall, at his expense, deliver to Buyer or his attorney, title insurance commitment with fee owner's titled policy premium to be paid by Seller at closing.

FIGURE 7.1 *Contract for Sale and Purchase (Continued)*

V. TIME FOR ACCEPTANCE AND EFFECTIVE DATE: If this offer is not executed by both of the parties within seven (7) days, the aforesaid deposit(s) shall be, at the option of Buyer, returned to him and this offer shall thereafter be null and void. The date of Contract ("Effective Date") shall be the date when the last one of the Seller and Buyer has signed this offer.

VI. CLOSING DATE: This transaction shall be closed and the deed and other closing papers delivered on or before ninety (90) days after the acceptance of this contract by Seller, unless extended by other provisions of Contract.

VII. OCCUPANCY: Seller represents that there are no parties in occupancy other than Seller, but if the property is intended to be rented or occupied beyond closing, the fact and terms thereof shall be stated herein, and the tenant(s) shall be disclosed pursuant to Standard G. Seller agrees to deliver occupancy of Property at time of closing unless otherwise specified below. If occupancy is to be delivered prior to closing, Buyer assumes all risk of loss to Property from date of occupancy, shall be responsible and liable for maintenance thereof from said date, and shall be deemed to have accepted the Property, real and personal, in its existing condition as of time of taking occupancy unless otherwise noted in writing.

VIII. TYPEWRITTEN OR HANDWRITTEN PROVISION: Typewritten or handwritten provisions inserted herein or attached hereto as Addenda shall control all printed provisions in conflict therewith.

THIS IS INTENDED TO BE A LEGALLY BINDING CONTRACT. IF NOT FULLY UNDERSTOOD, SEEK THE ADVICE OF AN ATTORNEY PRIOR TO SIGNING.

Witnesses: (Two recommended but NOT Required) Executed by Buyer on

(Buyer)

(Buyer)

Witnesses: (Two recommended but NOT Required) Executed by Seller on

(Seller)

(Seller)

FIGURE 7.1 *Contract for Sale and Purchase (Continued)*

NEGOTIATION FEE: Seller agrees to pay the real estate firm named below at the time of closing, from the disbursements of the proceeds of sale, compensation in the amount of _____% of the gross purchase price or $_____ , for its services in effecting the sale by finding a Buyer ready, willing, and able to purchase pursuant to the foregoing Contract.

(Name of Firm)   (Seller)

(Representative)   (Seller)

STANDARDS FOR REAL ESTATE TRANSACTIONS

A. EVIDENCE OF TITLE: A title insurance commitment shall be issued by a qualified title insurer agreeing to issue to Buyer, upon recording of the deed to Buyer, an owner's policy insurance in the amount of the purchase price, insuring title of the Buyer to the property, subject to liens, encumbrances or qualifications set forth in this Contract and those which shall be discharged by the Seller at or before closing. Buyer shall have 30 days from date of receiving evidence of title to examine same. If title is found defective, Buyer shall, within 3 days thereafter, notify Seller in writing specifying defect(s). If said defect(s) render title unmarketable, Seller shall have 120 days from receipt of notice within which to remove said defect(s), and if Seller is unsuccessful in removing them within said time, Buyer shall have the option of either (1) accepting the title as it then is, (2) demanding a refund of all monies paid hereunder which shall forthwith be returned to Buyer and thereupon Buyer and Seller shall be released, as to one another, of all further obligations under the Contract. However, Seller agrees that he will, if title is found to be unmarketable, use diligent effort to correct the defect(s) in title within the time provided therefore, including the bringing of necessary suits.

B. EXISTING LIENS: Seller shall furnish a statement from the lien holder setting forth principal balance, method of payment, interest rate, prepayment penalty guidelines and whether the loan is in good standing. If a loan requires approval of the Buyer by the lender in order to avoid default, or for assumption by the Buyer of said loan, and (1) the lender does not approve the Buyer, the Buyer may rescind the Contract, or (2) require an increase in the interest rate or charge a fee for any reason in excess of $100.00. The Buyer may rescind the Contract unless Seller elects to pay such increase or excess or Seller and Buyer shall each pay 50% of such fee. Buyer shall use reasonable diligence to obtain approval.

FIGURE 7.1 *Contract for Sale and Purchase (Continued)*

C. PURCHASE MONEY NOTES: The purchase money note, if any, shall provide a 30-day grace period in the event of default if it is a first-position loan and a 15-day grace period if a second-position loan; shall provide for right of prepayment in whole or in part without penalty, shall not provide for acceleration or interest adjustment in event of resale of the Property; and shall be otherwise in form and content as required by Seller's attorney; provided, however, Seller may only require clauses customarily found in notes generally utilized by savings and loan institutions in the county wherein the Property is located. Buyer shall require all prior lien and encumbrances to be kept in good standing and forbid modifications of or future advances under prior mortgage(s).

D. SURVEY: The buyer, within time allowed for delivery of evidence of title and examination thereof, may have the Property surveyed at his expense. If the survey, certified by a registered surveyor, shows any encroachment of said Property, or that improvements intended to be located on the Property in fact encroach on lands of others, or violate any of the Contract covenants, the same shall be treated as a title defect.

E. TERMITES: The Seller within time allowed for delivery of evidence of title and examination thereof, or no later than 10 days prior to closing, whichever date occurs last, must have improvements inspected at the Seller's expense by a Certified Pest Control Operator to determine whether there is any visible active termite infestation or visible existing damage from termite infestation in the improvements. If Seller is informed of either or both of the foregoing, Seller will have 4 days from date of written notice thereof or 2 days after selection of a contractor, whichever occurs first, within which to have all damages, whether visible or not, inspected and estimated by a licensed building or general contractor. Seller shall pay valid cost of treatment and repair of all damage up to $1\frac{1}{2}\%$ of Purchase Price. Should such cost exceed the amount, Buyer shall have the option of canceling Contract within the 5 days after receipt of contractor's repair estimate by giving written notice to Seller, or Buyer may elect to proceed with the transaction in which event Buyer shall receive a credit at closing in the amount equal to $1\frac{1}{2}\%$ of said Purchase Price. "Termites" shall be deemed to include all wood-destroying organisms.

F. INGRESS AND EGRESS: Seller warrants that there is ingress and egress to the Property sufficient for the intended use hereof the title to which is in accordance with Standard.

FIGURE 7.1 *Contract for Sale and Purchase (Continued)*

G. LEASES: Seller shall, not less than 15 days prior to closing, furnish to Buyer copies of all written leases and estoppel letters from each tenant specifying the nature and duration of said tenant's occupancy, rental rates and advanced rent and security deposits paid by tenant. In the event Seller is unable to obtain such letter from each tenant, the same information shall be furnished by Seller to Buyer within said time period in the form of a Seller's affidavit, the Buyer may thereafter contact tenants to confirm such information. Seller shall deliver and assign all original leases to Buyer at closing.

H. LIENS: Seller shall, both as to the Property and personality being sold here-under, furnish to Buyer at time of closing an affidavit attesting to the absence, unless otherwise provided for herein, of any financing statement, claims of lien or potential lien holders known to Seller and further attesting that there have been no improvements to the Property for 90 days immediately preceding date of closing. In addition to Seller's lien affidavit setting forth the names of all such general contractors, subcontractors, suppliers, and material men and further re-citing that in fact all bills for work to the Property which could serve as a basis for a mechanic's lien have been paid or will be paid at closing.

I. PLACE OF CLOSING: Closing shall be held in county wherein Property is lo-cated, at the office of attorney or other closing agent designated by Buyer.

J. TIME: Time is of the essence of the Contract. Any reference herein to time periods of less than 6 days shall in the computation thereof exclude Saturdays, Sundays, and legal holidays, and any time period provided for herein which shall end on a Saturday, Sunday, or legal holiday shall extend to 5:00 pm of the next full business day.

K. EXPENSES: State documentary stamps that are required to be affixed to the instrument of conveyance, intangible tax on and recording of purchased money note to Seller, and cost of recording any corrective instruments shall be paid by Seller. Documentary stamps to be affixed to the note or notes secured by the purchase money note and cost of recording the deed and financing statements shall be paid by Seller.

L. SPECIAL ASSESSMENT LIENS: Certified, confirmed, and ratified special as-sessment liens as of date of closing (and not as of Effective Date) are to be paid by Seller. Pending liens as of date of closing shall be assumed by Buyer, provided, however, that the improvement has been substantially completed as of the Effec-tive Date. Such pending liens shall be considered as certified, confirmed, or rat-ified and Seller shall, at closing, be charged an amount equal to the last estimate by the public body of the assessment for the improvement.

FIGURE 7.1 *Contract for Sale and Purchase (Continued)*

M. PERSONAL PROPERTY INSPECTION, REPAIR: Seller warrants that all major appliances, heating, cooling, electrical, plumbing system, and machinery are in working condition as of 6 days prior to closing. Buyer may, at his expense, have inspections made of said items by licensed person dealing in the repair and maintenance thereof, and shall report in writing to Seller such items as found not in working condition prior to taking of possession thereof, or 6 days prior to closing, whichever is first. Unless Buyer reports failures within said period, he shall be deemed to have waived Seller's warranty as to failures not reported. Valid reported failures shall be corrected at Seller's cost with funds thereof escrowed at closing. Seller agrees to provide access for inspection upon reasonable notice.

N. RISK OF LOSS: If the improvements are damaged by fire or other casualty prior to closing, and cost of restoring same does not exceed 3% of the Assessed Valuation of the improvements so damaged, cost of restoration shall be an obligation of the Seller and closing shall proceed pursuant to the terms of Contract with cost therefore escrowed at closing. In the event the cost of repair or restoration exceeds 3% of the assessed valuation of the improvements so damaged, Buyer shall have the option of either taking the Property as is, together with either the said 3% or any insurance proceeds payable by virtue of such loss or damaged or of canceling Contract and receiving return of deposit(s) made hereunder.

O. PROCEEDS OF SALE AND CLOSING PROCEDURE: The deed shall be recorded upon clearance of funds, if abstract, evidence of title continue at Seller's expense to show title to Buyer, without any encumbrances or change which would render Seller's title unmarketable from the date of the last evidence, and the cash proceeds of sale shall be held in escrow by Seller's attorney or by such other escrow agent as may be mutually agreed upon for a period of not longer than 5 days from and after the closing date. If Seller's title is rendered unmarketable, Buyers shall within 5 day period, notify Seller in writing of the defect and Seller shall have 30 days from date of receipt of such notification to cure said defect. In the event Seller fails to timely cure said defect, all monies paid hereunder shall, upon written demand therefore and within 5 days thereafter be returned to Buyer and, simultaneously with such repayment, Buyer shall vacate the Property and reconvey same to the Seller by special warranty deed. In the event Buyer fails to make timely demand for refund, Buyer shall take title to such intervening defect except as may be available to Buyer by virtue of warranties, if any, contained in deed. If a portion of the purchase price is to be derived from institutional financing or refinancing, the requirements of the lending institution

FIGURE 7.1 *Contract for Sale and Purchase (Continued)*

as to place, time of day, and procedure for closing, and for disbursement of mortgage proceeds shall control anything in this Contract to the contrary notwithstanding. Provided, however, that the Seller shall have the right to require from such lending institution at closing a commitment that it will not withhold disbursement of loan proceeds as a result of any title defect attributable to Buyer-mortgagor.

P. PRORATIONS AND INSURANCE: Assessed taxes, rent, interest, insurance, and other expenses, and revenue of the Property shall be prorated as of date of closing. Buyer shall have the option of taking over any existing policies of insurance on the Property, if assumable, in which event premiums shall be prorated. The cash at closing shall be increased or decreased as may be required by said prorations. All references in Contract to prorations as of date of closing will be deemed "date of occupancy" if occupancy occurs prior to closing, unless otherwise provided for herein.

Q. CONVEYANCE: Seller shall convey title to the Property by statutory warranty deed. Personal property shall, by the request of Buyer, be conveyed by an absolute bill of sale with warranty of title, subject to such liens as may be otherwise provided for herein.

REVIEWING THE SAMPLE CONTRACT

Let's go through my sample Contract for Sale and Purchase line by line so you understand what each is for.

Parties, as "Seller"—This refers to the person or name of corporation selling the property.

"of"—Fill in the contact information of the seller here. It's not necessarily the property address. You need a physical address, not a P.O. Box, to get legal papers to the seller. You also need a phone number for reaching him or her.

"and, as "Buyer"—Use your corporation name here

"of"—Your contact information

Part I: Description—Any blank for which you have no information yet, fill in with "N/A," which means Not Applicable. Many people leave blanks empty on contracts. I won't sign contracts that have blanks because things can be added in later, plus I don't know whether the others involved saw that blank. However, when you fill in a blank with N/A, they know you saw it; the information asked simply doesn't apply.

 a. County
 b. The physical address of the property
 c. When buying commercial property, you can use a general boilerplate answer for this: "Any and all utilities on the property at acceptance of offer that are needed for continued use."

Part II: Purchase Price—"See offers A, B, and C." This is your boilerplate answer. I'll explain these offers later in this chapter.

 a. Deposit—Put any amount in there, but make it at least $100. That's considered an appropriate exchange for real property. If you need to put more money down to make the deal, you can use a promissory note. Now, if a great deal comes up and the seller insists on more cash down than your standard $100, by all means consider and comply. My whole approach is speed. I tell sellers, "Look, if we do this quickly enough, the check won't even have time to clear in the escrow account before we close, so why even bother?"

 b. "Loans in favor of" refers to the name of the bank or lender who has the existing loan on the property. Usually, there will be a loan on the property, which you likely will be trying to take over.

"Bearing interest at"—List the interest rate.

"Payable as to principal and interest"—Record the principal and interest payment.

 c. "Purchase money note" is the formal term for seller financing. You'll want to call it by its formal term; you'll see why when we get to the A, B, C section. Put N/A in this blank.

 d. "Balance to close"—Fill this in with N/A because the seller will need to look at your three offers first.

This contract can become your boilerplate and should take less than four minutes to fill out. If you don't know the seller's name, rather than leaving the first blank empty, use "associated with . . . (name of brokerage firm)" and the firm's contact information. You can also call the broker and ask for the seller's name. Often, brokers won't give it to you, so tell them, "I'm sending over a noncircumvention, nondisclosure agreement. Sign it and then you can give me the name." It's that easy.

Part IV: Having the seller provide and pay for the title evidence saves you time and money.

Part V: You can change the number of days in your boilerplate. Students new to investing often feel more comfortable with seven days. Then, after they get tired of waiting by the phone to hear if the offer has been accepted, they change it to two to three days. I like to keep it between 24 and 48 hours.

Part VI: You can change the number of days here too. The note boxed in after Part VIII is not needed legally, but I include it as a courtesy to the seller. If sellers get into an argument with you about the contract, and they go to a court of law saying they didn't understand what it meant, the judge will respond with "Ignorance is no excuse for breaking the law." The boxed notice is an added reminder.

"Witnesses"—The witness sees that you signed the contract. That person doesn't need to know what it is and is not legally bound to anything.

Note: I like to move this signature section to the end of the contract so the sellers have to read through everything before they get to it. That way, they are aware that they are bound to *everything* that's in print, not just the print above their signatures.

Note: In STANDARDS FOR REAL ESTATE TRANSACTIONS, under B.

"Existing Liens"—This means you don't have to do a title search.

Noncircumvention, Nondisclosure Agreement

"Noncircumvention" means a prospective buyer can't go around you and approach the seller directly. You can have the buyer sign it for each deal or for all the deals you present. (As a protection, I always have it apply to all deals that I show them for all eternity.)

Here's how circumvention works. You talk to a prospect about buying a piece of property, saying, "It's a great property. It's $4.25 million and it's worth $6 million."

"Great! I want to see it," the person responds.

"Okay, here's the address. Go look at it."

With the address in hand, the prospective buyer can go to the courthouse and find out who owns it. Then he can go directly to the seller and offer more, say $4.5 million for the property. That implies that the seller just let your deal fall through. The noncircumvention agreement keeps that from happening.

Although noncircumvention keeps prospective buyers from going around the broker to the seller and working a better deal after they know what the seller will agree to, the nondisclosure stops them from telling someone else. In effect, it prevents another party from getting in touch with the seller on their behalf.

These two agreements work hand in hand. (You can get various versions of these agreements online by going to a search engine and typing in "Noncircumvention, nondisclosure agreement.")

Addenda to the Purchase Contract

I've added numerous addenda to the purchase contract I use. (Go to my Web site at http://www.LargeRealEstate.com.) Although the points are written in fancy language, they're all based on one idea: "I will buy your property unless I change my mind."

You can pick and choose which addenda you want to include in your contract:

Addenda

- Buyer has the right to personally inspect and give his or her written approval of the described property within 7 days after the acceptance of this contract by the Seller.
- Buyer has the right to assign this contract.
- Buyer has the right to full inspection of the property within 48 hours prior to closing.
- Purchaser shall have the right at the termination of this agreement to renew, for a like period, under the terms contained herein.
- Any Escrow Account held by the mortgagee or trust company shall be conveyed with the property and is included in the purchase price.
- Seller's right to retain deposit money in the event of default by Buyer shall be in full settlement of any claims and shall be the Seller's sole remedy. Seller shall not be entitled to specific performance. If Seller defaults, Seller shall return Buyer's deposit plus an equal amount of his own money.
- Seller agrees to subordinate this purchase money mortgage to any new financing Buyer may place on the property at a future date and shall execute such documents as may be necessary to effect such subordination.
- This contract is contingent on an independent appraisal on the property in an amount not less than the purchase price.
- The purchase money note and mortgage shall be paid in equal annual payments.
- The total amount of the purchase money mortgage shall be divided into separate promissory notes for each year's payments.
- The Buyer reserves the right to substitute collateral securing the purchase money mortgage, said collateral to be

equal to or greater than owner's equity. Seller shall execute all documents necessary to do so.

- In the event Seller should elect to sell the purchase money mortgage at a later date, Buyer (maker) shall have the right of first refusal of any bona fide written offer.

- Seller shall notify maker (Buyer) at least 30 days prior to instituting any foreclosure privileges allowed by the purchase money note, by certified mail, and the maker shall have the right to cure the same.

- The property as described in the attached contract shall be the sole security for the purchase money note.

- Payments on purchase money mortgage shall not begin and interest shall not accrue until six (6) months after the closing date.

- This transaction is subject to Buyer's inspection and written acceptance of all the legal financial records and data of the Seller on the property (including but not limited to all leases, rent records, expense records, and tax returns regarding the property) for verification of representations of income and expenses.

- This transaction is subject to complete inspection of the property for compliance with the building, health, and fire codes, and Buyer's written acceptance of the condition of the premises. Seller shall correct all code violations.

- Seller warrants that all personal property, building structure, wiring, appliances, electrical fixtures, plumbing, heating, and air conditioning devices are in good operating condition and that the roof is in good repair and free of leaks, and all will be so at closing and for one (1) year after the date of closing. These warranties shall survive and extend past delivery of deed.

- Seller warrants there are no leases on the property for a period longer than six (6) months and no leases contain an option to renew on like terms.

- The Seller's purchase money mortgage shall be subordinate and inferior to any existing prior mortgage and to any extension, renewal, or replacement thereof.
- This transaction is subject to Buyer's inspection and written approval of terms of existing mortgages. This transaction is contingent on existing mortgages not having clauses providing for a balloon payment, balance due on sale or assumption or interest increase on sale, or assumption or prepayment penalty.
- Seller warrants that the information attached hereto as Addendum A is true and correct.
- Seller shall give Buyer a Bill of Sale for all personal property, and that part of the total purchase price attributable to personal property shall be determined by Buyer.
- Seller shall deliver to Buyer at closing a complete set of keys to the property, all insurance policies being assumed by the Buyer, copies of all mortgages assumed by the Buyer, copies of all mortgages assumed by the Buyer, all warranties and instructions on fixtures and personal property being sold, all leases and tenants' applications, all service contracts on property being sold, payment books on mortgages being assumed, and any blueprints or surveys regarding the property.
- Earnest money deposit shall be held in escrow by closing agent.
- The closing date shall be extended for all time necessary to cure title defects.
- All rights of grantee in this contract shall survive the passage of title and shall continue to exist after the deed is accepted.
- No monies shall be disbursed after closing until the deed is recorded and the title search updated to the recording of the deed.

- Buyer has the right to immediate possession of the property for purposes of making improvements and/or showing said property.
- All closing costs including prepaid items are to be paid by Seller.
- This transaction is subject to an inspection by any partner within three (3) days of the Seller's acceptance of the offer.
- The Seller agrees to hold a purchase money mortgage and further agrees that the maker of the promissory note reserves the right to miss one payment per loan year and failure to make such payment shall not be a default of the said note.

Reviewing Two Addenda to Purchase Contract

The first addendum reads:

"The Buyer has the right to personally inspect and give his or her written approval of the described property within seven (7) days after the acceptance of this contract by the Seller."

This means you don't even need to look at the property. You can go online, find a deal that looks good, and immediately write an offer. Once it's accepted, you have seven days to look at it and decide if you really want it.

In the beginning, however, I suggest you actually go and look at the properties you're interested in buying. Educate yourself on what they look like and how accurately they coincide with the written description. After a while, a property is a property; you just need to get the numbers. If the numbers work well, then send over different inspectors to be your "eyes."

The second addendum reads:

"The buyer has the right to assign this contract."

That means you can give the property to someone else. Once you get the property under contract, it's under your complete control. If the sellers object, then say, "I understand. One of the reasons I have that in there is because I'm probably going to structure another corporation. With this addendum in there, that allows this contract to go in without writing out a new contract." Did you notice how I started this out? "One of the reasons . . ." Obviously, you know that some of the other reasons include that you may assign it to someone else for cash. I don't mind doing this because it really doesn't matter to them after the sale. People just get wary of things like that. And in the end, a contract is a contract.

Addenda You Might Want to Use

I'd like to draw attention to these additional addenda that aren't included in the sample contract on my Web site.

One additional addendum reads:

"The Buyer has an unlimited number of extensions in lieu of x% of total purchase price to be applied to purchase price at closing."

In addition to "I will buy your property unless I change my mind," this means that if you need an extension, you'll just buy it; you don't need to ask for it; "x%" means you use whatever percentage you decide to write into the contract.

For example, if you have a smaller building, say it's worth $1 million and you're borrowing at 1 percent, then you're paying

$10,000 in interest. (You can also use 0.5 percent, .25 percent, etc.) If you want an extension on this loan, you put up a certain amount of money, and it goes toward your purchase price so you're not paying extra—if you close. If you don't close, the seller gets to keep that money.

That's not a hazard and let me explain why. Let's say you put in 1 percent. You could buy that building 1 percent at a time. Right? You've locked in that price. You could buy that building, paying $10,000 each month, while hiring others to take care of it. Theoretically, this would be the model way to do it, but in practice you'll likely settle for three to four extensions. (Sometimes you'll face getting squeezed at closing. It's not uncommon to go to closing and find out that the lender has reevaluated the numbers and decided to change the terms.) This addendum lets you refuse the new terms and have another 30 days, giving you more room for negotiation.

The second new addendum reads:

> "The Buyer, upon acceptance of the contract, has final approval of all new tenants, new work, and any upgrades to purchase property."

That means that you have control of that property. What are you looking for? You want to make sure that one of the sellers' Uncle Mike doesn't all of a sudden get the deal of a lifetime with a two-year lease in your building where market rents are $1,000 a month and he's in there for $350. It happens. And often.

Here's another million-dollar addendum:

> "Any and all legal disputes arising from any part of this contract, property and thereof, will be settled in arbitration."

That means disputes won't be settled in court. Have you heard the common saying, "Nobody wins in a court of law?" Actually, the only people who win in court are lawyers. Consider this: A lawsuit is filed every 30 seconds in the United States. According to a top real estate attorney, average people will be sued four to five times over the course of their lifetime, and one of those cases will be devastating.

To prevent that probability, what do you do? You take a potential lawsuit out of the lawyers' hands and state that you'll settle disputes through arbitration. With arbitration, you state your case, the other person states his or her case, and the arbitrator rides the dispute down the middle. The arbitrator doesn't try to decide who's right and who's wrong but helps the opposing parties come to their own conclusions and agreements.

A, B, C OFFERS

Remember, for Part II: Purchase Price in your contract, you wrote, "See A, B, and C offers." What are these? They are three types of offers that I suggest you use.

The first type of offer that's sent to a seller is typically accepted 80 percent of the time. If the first offer isn't accepted, then 15 percent of the time the second offer is accepted, and a third offer is accepted 2 percent of the time. Together, that equals 97 percent. So 97 percent of the time, you can make deals happen with one of these three types of offers (C is a combination of A and B). It's wise to make all three of them and see which one suits the seller best.

Here's how it works with each of the three types of offers.

A offer: 100 percent seller financing. The A offer relates to 100 percent seller financing or PMM (PMM = purchase money mortgage). That's comparable to saying "I'll take over your payment, and you take care of the note or loan." When it comes to the note, a lot of times sellers are unwilling to accept an interest rate equal to present mortgage rates. Therefore, you'd want to raise the interest rate. In general, this A offer (depending on economic conditions and also location in the country) is not widely accepted by sellers. Nonetheless, it's wise to always make it an option, because it's a quick way to acquire an apartment building. If it's accepted, it works out extremely well. Here, because you are potentially giving two interest rates (one on the first mortgage and one on the second), make sure that you calculate the exact amount you're willing to pay.

This makes it necessary to understand what the net operating income (NOI) is, and then calculate how much interest you can pay the seller. Whenever you do this, always check the numbers. Calculate the payment at the agreed-on interest rate and make sure it cash flows. That's important. Just because you've got the formula right doesn't mean the numbers will still work!

How do you determine what you can pay to the seller? Remember, the maximum available, the NOI, is $2062.50. So add up the total payments—the first and the PMM—and make sure they're less than this number. You want them to cash flow.

B offer: All cash. The B offer is all cash. Where will you get the cash? Maybe out of your pocket but most likely from an investor. Use the maximum purchase price with positive cash flow or the lowest one of the numbers REAPAC™ calculated for you. Typically, you'll go with the cash flow number because it's the lowest dollar figure and gives you exactly what you want.)

Say the property you want to buy is worth $282,175. Can you offer less than that? Sure. Can you offer more than that? You'll lose money if you offer more because you want at least $1,000 positive cash flow. If you offer an amount higher than that, it's just eating out of your pocket. You've decided mathematically that's how much you need to buy this building, so that becomes your offer price.

C offer: Combo. The C offer, a combination of A and B, is at a price between A and B. You'll offer a little bit of cash, ask the seller to hold a little bit of the note, and take over the seller financing. Remember, the strategy of seller financing equates to cash to sellers. And that's out of your pocket, so you can offer a higher purchase price.

Looking at the two numbers from your A and B offers, you can take the average and come up with your C offer. Then you tell the sellers to refinance their note and you'll pay the difference. You could also put up some cash of your own. For example, you might take over their first mortgage, give them $70,000 cash, and handle the remaining balance in a note.

Where A, B, C Offers Come From

If you understand REAPAC™ or where you get the numbers from manually, you'll understand where you get your A, B, and C offers. You can make a ton of different A, B, C offers. This provides you with a boilerplate to use as a guideline.

Doing **C**alculations

When you analyze properties, you run the numbers or run them through REAPAC™ to get a number you can put in the offer.

Every partnership I set up on a piece of real estate is completely different. Although some common factors exist, I'm always dealing with human beings so nothing is standard. It's the same way with real estate—you're buying a building, but you're actually selling your ideas to those who own the building. To help these people understand exactly what you want to do with that property, start by gaining control of the situation through effective communication. But first, make sure you control the contract and that you grab the sellers' interest over other possible buyers.

Pay special attention to what you're communicating to the sellers through your contract. Sometimes your offer will be straightforward, focusing on the numbers. Other times your A, B, or C offer will look more like a manuscript, because you want to spell out the myriad benefits. Whatever you do is designed to capture the sellers' interest. They might not be interested in that specific deal, but they might become interested in what you're doing in your business overall, never having seen another person write an offer like that.

Without being able to open people's minds to a variety of possibilities, you won't be able to buy properties. It's as simple as that. You need to obtain money to buy properties so you can increase your net worth. You need to increase your net worth so you can buy larger properties. That's how climbing the ladder works in this business.

It all starts with writing offers. If you don't change what you're doing, things will just get worse. So through practice, consistency, and making lots of offers, you'll get there. Remember, in your business you're not buying "that" building; you're buying "a" building that fits your criteria and portfolio. Negotiate well to make that happen.

Two Types of Negotiators

There are two types of negotiators: those who are lowballers and those who are steadfast. Steadfast negotiators say "$145,363.11 and that's it. It's not negotiable; I'm not moving." A lowballer would start lower than that and be prepared to come up.

How do you choose your style? It usually depends on your personality.

I'm a lowballer, a trait that stems from when I was 17 years old. I wanted to buy a car, so I worked on a dockyard and saved $3,000 of my earnings. I was determined to get a Camaro—white with red vinyl interior—because it looked sharp. But I knew nothing about cars. Nothing at all, except that this kind of Camaro looked great. Its front hung low to the ground like a sports car should.

I found one Camaro being sold privately, and I went to see it. I fell in love with it! I walked around it kicking the tires because I thought, "If it was a bad car, the tires would fall off by kicking them hard enough." Then I stepped back a bit and really gave them a kick.

Can you believe it: I didn't even take the car for a test drive.

Still, I really wanted this car. So when it was time to negotiate the price, I took my stance. The seller wanted $3,500 for it. I said, "I'll give you $3,000." He said, "Okay," and ran in the house to write out the contract before I knew what was going on. It didn't take me long to realize I must have overpaid him for this car. But once I caught on to that, I didn't even renegotiate while he was writing up the contract.

I should have.

I got the car, drove it home, and quickly discovered it was missing a muffler and exhaust pipes. It cost me $450 to get these fixed. In addition, I wanted to put chrome rims on that baby so I decided I'd save money and do it myself. When I tried to jack up the car, the jack went right through the bottom of the undercarriage. I found out that the seller had attended Miami University in Miami, Florida, and the salty air there rusted the metal in the car right through. I also discovered the front was hanging low to the ground—like a sports car should, or so I thought—because it was missing five bolts.

Continued

Ever since then, I've learned to never allow my offer to be accepted on my first try. I never will. I became a lowballer, and I don't mind going as low as necessary. In fact, I don't mind going so low that the other person gets upset. When that happens, I've learned to make light of it and laugh my way out of an awkward situation. I'd rather do that than have the seller accept my offer right off the bat—like the guy who sold me the rusty Camaro.

For tips on negotiation, pick up a great book by Herb Cohen called *Negotiate This* or his earlier book called *You Can Negotiate Anything*. I've learned a lot from Cohen. He actually wrote these books for the FBI and CIA after training their agents. In fact, he has been involved in almost every major hostage negotiation conducted by the U.S. government and U.S. presidents.

WRITING OFFERS

The most important thing an investor does is write the contract/offer to buy a building, so don't spend too much time on other areas. Sure, you'll spend a lot of time at first talking to brokers, locating properties, and understanding the types of properties you want. Later, you'll streamline the offer process as soon as possible.

People often start out looking for a ten-unit apartment building; then they consider buying a warehouse; then they get into raw land development. It's easy to get sidetracked in this business because it's fun—especially when you recognize lots of different avenues to take and notice the few people taking them.

But once you get the process down—you're comfortable locating properties, talking to people in their language, and building your network of contacts—then you can branch out. Build a few apartment buildings, put in a park, develop some strip malls, and soon you're building a little town. You have the capability to do that.

DURING THE CALCULATION PHASE

People often slow down during the calculation phase because they want to get creative at that point. The creativity comes in the next step—how you structure your deals. So if the numbers tell you that you can buy a property for $174,958.11 with $1,000 cash flow, that number stays consistent. Punching in the numbers in REAPAC™ should take you only a few minutes. When people try to be creative this early in the game they get hurt. They wonder, "What if I could get an interest rate at x percent?" I suggest you just go with what you know you can do. And give yourself a cushion. Then if the broker says you can get a debt service at 6.5 percent, use 6.75 percent in your calculation. Interest rates can shift, as you know. If they go down, great—you just made a little extra money. But if they push up, you're protected.

Let's review the offers: A is 100 percent seller financing. B is cash. C is a combo of A and B. This combo can be structured many different ways and allows for lots of creativity.

I usually start by figuring the B offer first and then the A offer next. The C offer requires more thought, and I usually prefer it. Certainly I spend more time on the better deals when the sellers are clearly motivated and there's flexibility in the situation.

You can be sure to have the sellers' interest in the contract when they see the words "See attached." By writing that in, you're communicating that you're working on various options to get them interested.

After looking at the A (seller financing) and B (cash) offers, sellers know there is still another offer to look at: the C offer, which is usually the one most attractive for both of you. That's why I suggest you present them in that order. I've found that if you present the cash offer first, they'll only look at that and ignore the other two. You might even have cash as your C offer.

> ### P r i c e   o r   S p e e d — W h a t ' s   P r e f e r r e d ?
>
> Some people say you should always offer a lower amount than the one the seller wants. If you go through REAPAC™ and get your cash flow number, you will know if you can afford to pay that amount. Sometimes it will come out even above what the seller is asking. Why would you offer that? Because you want to get the transaction done quickly. Never lower a number just for the heck of it. Be strategic and rely on your calculations and good judgment.

Sample Analysis

Get the property setup sheet from a real estate broker and pull the appropriate numbers from it to make your calculations. For this example, you see a $50,000-a-year rent roll. From there you want to determine the GRM, which is the gross rent multiplier. This number is general but will give you a wealth of knowledge, and knowing it shows you to brokers and sellers as knowledgeable.

Remember that gross rent, gross income, and rent roll all mean the same thing—it's $50,000. When your GRM is at 6.0, it refers to low- to middle-income areas. It's also called C real estate, which means certain areas are characterized by people working hard with pride of ownership, even though they don't make a lot of money. As noted in Chapter 1, that's exactly the kind of area you want for your investments.

Note: A GRM at 6.1 to 9 is middle-income to upper-middle-income area, which is B real estate. A GRM of 9.1+ indicates A areas, or upper-income properties.

To determine the GRM number for this example, take the asking price of $300,000, divide it by the gross income (rent roll), and you get a multiplier number. In this case, $50,000 goes into $300,000 six times, so this property has a multiplier of six (6.0).

That means it's in that C area that you want to invest in. (If you get 10 or 12 for a GRM, then you know you're looking at high-income areas. You can figure out where the property is just by taking the purchase price and dividing it by the income. Conversely, you can also determine what the price should be by multiplying the income by the GRM multiplier.)

What does "six times rent roll" actually mean? It means there is low appreciation and high income. It also indicates that those properties won't double in value in the next year. Typically, they grow at an average of 5 percent a year. It can still work for you, though. You just might hit a home run if the area grows or a shopping mall comes in. Then the appreciation on your building can go through the roof overnight. It happens but not often. Be aware that when you talk to brokers about finding a property at six times rent roll or less, you've provided them with a lot of information. They know you want C paper and you're looking for a building with high cash flow.

Differences between Properties

Rents don't change that much in C properties. With Section 8, the government has to make sure these people are housed, so they offer competitive rents. But because the price of the building is lower, your expenses tend to be low, and therefore you're not paying that much money for a building that generates good money.

B properties have average appreciation and average cash flow. You won't have as much cash flow as you will with C properties because your building costs more. But B properties are usually located in a better area, so you'll realize a higher appreciation.

A properties are the "trophy" properties—the mansions and buildings in prime areas. They have extremely high appreciation and low-to-negative cash flow. That means when you buy an A building, you won't make money until you sell it. In fact, you will incur a lot of costs to hold it and work on it, so know that you'll lose money until you sell it.

Most investors are looking in the middle—at properties with a GRM of eight (8.0) and higher. Then they tell me they don't have cash flow, but they want a nice building so they can drive by with their friends and say, "Hey, I own that building."

You can do that with C property too—just drive fast! However, I don't know any successful real estate investor who didn't own middle- to low-income properties as a base to get started. Most of these investors still own C properties; they just don't talk about it. Some even think of them as charity, but they still provide a solid base because that's where their money comes from.

INTEREST RATES AND CREDIT SCORES

What interest rate do you use on REAPAC™ when plugging in the information? Use the interest rate that you, personally, will be able to get from a lender. First, check your credit rating by going to http://www.myfico.com to get your FICO scores from the three credit agencies. (This Web site also tells you how to increase your FICO score and how certain purchases and actions increase or decrease your score. Note: Checking your credit at http://www .myfico.com doesn't decrease your rating as other avenues of checking credit do.) My Web site http://www.LargeRealEstate .com can offer further credit solutions.

Your FICO score is the dominant factor that lenders use to assess your creditworthiness, and its name is derived from Fair Isaac Corp., the firm that developed the scoring model. Scores range from 350 to 800; generally a good score is 720 and above. Therefore, if your credit score is 650, you'll be able to qualify for a good interest rate and possibly have some leverage to negotiate an even better rate.

The brokers most likely work with the middle score. Realize that the three credit agencies just report the information they receive, yet it's amazing how differently each of them reports and rates things. Be sure to check both your personal and business credit reports.

After gathering this credit information, go to a mortgage broker who can give you a range of possible interest rates. If you want specific numbers, go to a lender and apply to prequalify or get preapproved for a loan.

What's the difference between the two?

- Getting prequalified gives you a general idea of what you can borrow.
- Getting preapproved means the bankers have checked your credit and determined exactly how much you can borrow and at what rate.

If you have bad personal credit, first pay off your bills or at least pay them down. Then get a collateralized loan. Go to a bank, put $1,000 in a savings account, and then borrow it back. You'll be charged 8 percent interest. The paperwork says this doesn't help repair credit, but in effect it does. Call to make sure the bank reports this so it serves to increase your credit score.

STRUCTURING YOUR BUSINESS

With commercial property, most investors set up a corporate structure and obtain nonrecourse loans, which means that if the loan defaults, the lenders can't attach personal assets to recover the debt. (Beware: Banks question an investor's morals if he or she goes into high-risk ventures with the attitude that because only a few deals will make money, the investor can walk away from some debts to make up for the ones that don't work. Specifically, such an investor risks having the bank take back the property.)

I recommend structuring each property as a separate corporation rather than putting several buildings under the umbrella of one corporation. Then if something unforeseen occurs and one of your buildings doesn't yield the income you want, only one of your buildings—and the people who live and work there—are affected. If all your buildings were under the umbrella of one corporation, you risk having a bad deal bring down all the buildings under that corporation. When income from one of several buildings can't cover the mortgage, lenders who financed the other buildings accelerate the notes payable, thus jeopardizing the profitability of all the buildings within that corporate structure. Be sure to protect your business wisely.

8

FORMING PARTNERSHIPS

How do you know who's going to be a good partner in your real estate business and what you'll get from the partnership?

In my opinion, partnerships are one of the most misunderstood aspects of business. They're fairly simple; the problems come when emotions get involved and a deal goes bad. Putting everything in writing is the best way to keep a partnership simple but successful. Always have contracts; mistakes most often occur as a result of the failure to get agreements in writing.

PARTNERSHIPS: EXCHANGE BASED

People often think partnerships are based on money, but they're really all about exchange.

Partnership = Exchange

When you approach a partner, you want to set up an exchange. You're bringing your knowledge of how to put a deal together and make the numbers work. In many instances, that type of knowledge can be more valuable than cold, hard cash. I don't mean to downplay the value of investors' funds, but never underestimate the knowledge you bring to put the deal together. Without that, quite frankly, there would be no deal to put money into. And truly, all money is, in itself, a form of exchange. Do you see that if you exchange money and knowledge, you're actually putting together a partnership?

A Team of Roverbacks

I used to play football for Temple University in Philadelphia, Pennsylvania, on Temple's Division I team (which means you'd see my team playing on national TV). Division I teams often have the best players in the country and you can bet each player is big in size, though I was among the smallest.

We'd play spring ball early in the year to practice before the football season actually started. I think spring ball is a longer and tougher period than the season itself because we'd practice for four hours or more at a pop. I played as a "roverback" (or "rover"), which was a great position because I'd get to go to the side of the field where all the action took place.

One day, our group of roverbacks was tired and missed a lot of tackles. Our coach said we were bringing down the team, so he designed a drill especially for us to toughen us up. It's been handed down to subsequent teams as the legendary Junction Drill. Here's how it worked.

Playing defense, we had a tight end, fullback, and halfback. No other players were on the field except for them and the quarterback. The drill gave us three options: first, the tight end would come out to catch a pass, and we'd have to defend against him or tackle him.

Playing the second option, this tight end would hit us roverbacks and block us. That would be a running play. We had to hit him, shed him, and get ready for a run. Then the fullback, at 6'3" and 265 pounds, would come at us. If he got the ball, we were to tackle him. If he didn't have the ball, we'd go to the player behind him, who weighed a mere 185 pounds but was a runner-up Heisman Trophy winner.

In the third option, we were to hit the tight end, who weighed 285 pounds, then run and hit the fullback's 265 pounds (he had a ten-yard running start) and push him into the runner. So we had our work cut out for us.

Thirteen of us played roverback position. Once we started the drill, we quickly learned how painful it was! It was even painful for those watching from the sidelines. One by one, all the spectators left.

This drill certainly toughened us up. In fact, it physically injured ten players who couldn't play for a week. After two weeks of doing the drill, the remaining three roverbacks got together and decided we wouldn't take it anymore. We made this plan: We'd go after one guy, the fullback, hit him as hard as we could and bury him. After the third hit, they saw we were serious. In this way, we evened the playing field.

We turned the tables because we decided to work together as partners. This partnership, which came out of a painful experience, enabled us to dominate in that drill.

That's an example of how to think of successful partnerships. Look at them as an accumulation of forces—knowledge, money, and intelligence. Clearly, people work better when they "play" as a team.

WHEN TO USE A PARTNERSHIP

There are times you will use a partnership and other times you won't. I try to set up a partnership whenever possible. But be clear about this: If you're going to work with a partner, it should be to make your enterprise bigger than it already is. If you bring on a partner to continue the status quo, that's a sign that something is structurally wrong. So if you're buying a building every three months but need to bring in a partner to continue that pace, that's not a good sign. Alternately, if your goal is to buy a building every month, then bringing in a partner becomes an asset. Similarly, you can use a partner to take on projects that require a lot of rehab. Ideally, therefore, partners help you grow and do larger and larger transactions.

As you know, I suggest you start with 10 to 25 units. I keep mentioning that because I want to hammer the point home—it's not about starting small but about building momentum.

As you start off with that many units, you might have the personal capacity to put down $35,000 as payment into the deal and have another $10,000 for any added expenses. But let's say you find a 10-unit property that needs $200,000 in rehab. I'd suggest that, as a beginner, you stay away from a deal like that unless you can bring in a partner who has the money to support it because of the holding costs—taxes, insurance, maintenance, and the like—as you do the rehab. Even if that property could potentially bring in a windfall when it's ready, it's still dangerous to leverage your finances that much when you're just starting as an investor.

HOW TO CHOOSE A PARTNER

Your partner is defined as anyone who puts money into a deal, whether it's the Bank of America or your favorite uncle. You're always better off setting up a limited partnership and giving your partners more information than they need, especially in the beginning. Most people do the opposite—they try to give partners as little information as possible at first because they don't want their investment partners to become too involved. I think you're better off inundating them with information, yet it still depends on the type of partnership you set up—direct or indirect.

Remember, your lenders are your partners, so keep them in the information loop. Let them know what's going on. Send them

Beware **t**he **G**reed **F**actor

Many things can happen in the course of rehabbing a building. In fact, my father, Frank Warr, who owns an architectural firm, brought this point to my attention when I considered buying a $5 million property. It needed extensive rehab, but I thought I could get money from the lender and do a 100 percent financing deal on it. My father posed the following question: "What happens if, in the middle of the rehab, something unexpected comes up? Do you have the money to pay for that?" I didn't. "Well, what do you think would happen to the deal if a crisis occurred?"

"Well, I couldn't finish the rehab; then I'd miss mortgage payments and possibly foreclose on it." As soon as I answered that question, I saw what he was getting at. Greed had entered into this deal as a grim factor.

This scenario happens to many people. I wanted to do the deal, keep all the profits—and be a hero to myself. But my father showed me that greed was making me risk a lot more than the potential reward. Instead, I looked at it like this: If I pull off the deal and do it myself, I'll make a lot of money. If something goes wrong with the deal, I won't make money—in fact, I'd probably lose money. That's feast or famine. But then I realized if I brought in a business partner, I'd be able to do the deal, make money on it, and get a few good nights of sleep in the meantime.

quarterly reports on how profitable the building is. In the beginning, deal with smaller banks and later graduate to larger banks.

If you prefer to get seller financing, also approach the sellers as partners. When I present my offer, I say, "Now that we're going to be partners on the building . . ." I like to state my offers to the sellers as if what I want to happen has already come to pass. For example, say, "Here's what I want you to do. I want you to refinance this property. You have a $600,000 first mortgage. You should borrow $800,000. That means you'll pocket $200,000 and hold the note for $200,000. Now that we're partners on this and you have $200,000 invested, I'm going to send you the quarterly reports. Where do you want those to be mailed?" See how you can pull the sellers into the deal in this way?

The Importance of Communication

Let's say you've got $200,000 that you give to an investment company to invest in an annuity and some mutual funds. Your representative says, "In 30 years, we'll give you a lump-sum payment." And you say, "Okay, when will I get statements?" If the response is "We just don't bother with that. We told you we'd give you the payment. We have other things to do," then you wouldn't be too happy with the investment company.

It's the same with people with whom you do seller financing. Keep them in touch with details about the property and offer them quarterly reports. In the beginning, they might request monthly reports. After a while, send them only an annual report.

Keeping sellers/partners apprised of the situation often produces a higher closure rate on seller financing than would occur if you neglect to do this. The last thing you want to do is alienate the sellers by saying, "Look, just take the note. It's quick and easy for you, and you can go about doing your business. You don't have to worry about it again." Well, the sellers do worry about it. After all, it's $200,000 of their money. And it's their building that they might have to take back. So make sure they're comfortable right from the beginning.

Remember, you can write up your agreement in one of three ways: percentage (a flat percentage interest rate return), equity (an equity owner, often 50-50 on a specific property), or combo (combination of percentage and equity).

Doctors as Partners

I've talked about partnerships in general and how to use the money, knowledge, and experience you get from them. But whom do you actually approach?

Doctors are my first pick when it comes to partners, because they typically have what you're looking for: a lot of money and little time. Usually doctors make good money and are able to save a decent amount. Part of the downside of their high earnings is their having little time to buy real estate on their own. In addition, because they make a lot of money, they have a big problem to deal with—paying lots of taxes. And that's a problem you can help solve.

Real estate is an ideal vehicle for doctors to invest in. In your partnership, you'll form a corporation, which helps them save on taxes. Also, a partner is entitled to depreciation on a property, which can bring down investing doctors' taxable income. A third factor is tax credits. Tax credits are actual dollar-for-dollar credits issued by the federal government for upkeep on middle- to low-income properties.

Investors and the Federal Government

At one time, the federal government tried to set up a system of housing people. It didn't work, and the federal government soon discovered that real estate investors had the capability to house people successfully. The government had to figure out how to get investors to do its job for it, deciding to give them incentives such as guaranteed subsidies, decreased property taxes, and tax credits.

Therefore, if doctors become your partners and put cash into the partnership, they have their choice. They can either get a cash return, which most doctors don't want, or they can receive tax credits, which they usually do want. This is what I call a win-win situation. Having partners put up the money to fix a building so it can make more money and not require cash from you—that's a win for you. And the doctors want the so-called loss or tax advantage—that's a win for them.

Tax Advantages in Two Ways

Remember that you have tax advantages with corporations as well as with real estate. When you combine the two, you have a powerful entity. But keep in mind the difference between tax evasion and tax advantages. The difference is intent. If you enter into a partnership or form a corporation for no other reason than to lower your taxes, that's tax evasion and it's illegal. If, however, you set up a corporation or partnership with the intent to make money, make your business profitable, employ a few people, and save on taxes (thus increasing your income), that's called tax advantages and it's legal.

In situations where doctors are investors, their intent is to make a lot of money—and part of that intent is achieved because the law allows them to pay less money in taxes on income resulting from their investments and tax credits. But they're actually postponing a certain amount of income until after they sell the buildings they've invested in. That means temporarily they receive tax credits to offset other income, but in the long term they'll receive money in a lump-sum payment called capital gains.

This demonstrates another way that partnerships work; it's not always a cash for cash situation.

Contractors as Partners

Investors like doing business with contractors, too. As my mentor told me, "There are two types of contractors; those who are real estate investors and those who want to be." Contractors fix up apartment buildings, spending a lot of time and effort on high-quality workmanship for a salary and at the same time watching the investors make a fortune on deals. That can be demoralizing because they know that the buildings appreciated in value as a result of their work. They feel they should be compensated by more than just their salary. If you ask any contractor who has become a real estate investor, I'll bet, 99 times out of 100, that factor has been the motivator for them.

Investing with a Contractor

I had placed an ad in the newspaper that read, "Real estate investor needs to buy 100+-unit apartment building in the next 30 days." As you can probably tell, I was motivated to find something fast because I was sitting on an investor's cash and wanted to spend it quickly. From the ad, a contractor named Mike, who was also a real estate investor, contacted me. He was looking to form a partnership given the right investment opportunity. After deciding to work together, we set up a partnership this way: I ran ads in the paper, looked for apartment buildings, and analyzed; he inspected the buildings I found. This approach did break my usual formula, which is to write offers on properties before inspecting them. Only once an offer was accepted would I hire an inspector or contractor to look at the property. That formula typically saves me time and effort. But this new scenario worked well because when I found a deal we liked, Mike inspected the building right away, wrote a report, and told me how much he was willing to invest in it. That allowed me to go back with full knowledge of what the property looked like and structure the offer based on his professional opinion. Our combination of skills and talents made this a good partnership.

I like having contractors as partners because I find that, like doctors, they put aside money for real estate investments. They clearly intend to make more money and move beyond general contracting. Another obvious advantage is their ability to do any work or rehab that an investment property needs. They're also able to monitor construction at a property, which is an extremely valuable asset to have in a partner. Remember, contractors enjoy the cash flow from their investment and can get tax credits just as doctors do.

Lawyers and CPAs as Partners

I also like to partner with lawyers and certified public accountants (CPAs) because of their professional knowledge but, more than that, because of their databases. If you get in touch with CPAs or attorneys about a potential real estate deal, they may be able to complete the deal themselves and make the money. If they're not able to, they have clients who might be appropriate to work with.

Why would lawyers or CPAs suggest that one of their clients be your business partner instead of them? First, by introducing you to a client of theirs, they can get a finder's fee. Also, the association with you can result in more legal and accounting business for them.

For example, if you complete a deal with a CPA's client, then that CPA will likely want to do all the accounting and corporate work for the corporation and that building. That means he or she will be getting a finder's fee and a new client (the new corporation) as well. The same holds true for attorneys; they receive a finder's fee plus doing any legal and court work needed by the client/property owner. It's a win-win for all parties.

Number of Partners

When you do partnership agreements, you're better off involving five partners (you plus four others) or fewer. Anything more than five partners could make it an exchange-traded vehicle

> **F** *i n d e r ' s* **F** *e e s*
>
> Who decides how much a finder's fee should be? You, the investor. Typically, it's a percentage of the amount of money invested in the deal and is around 2.5 percent. That means if $100,000 is invested, the finder's fee would be $2,500.

that's regulated by the Securities and Exchange Commission (SEC), a government agency that regulates stocks and bonds. If this is the route you want to take with five or more partners, then I suggest you consult a professional to set this up. Generally, because it's simpler than dealing with several people, I prefer to deal with only one person in a partnership, which is good advice for you too.

Say a number of people come to you wanting to pool their money. Six of them put in $50,000 each for a total of $300,000. How would you deal with this situation? You could tell them, "Form a partnership. Structure it the way you want. If you want to talk to my attorney for advice and help to set it up, go ahead. Determine how you're splitting the money and how a buyout will work, in case one or more partners want to get out of the partnership."

Once these partners work out the legal details, then you can deal with the entity they've just formed. This keeps your partnership agreement limited to a single one while still making room for many people. I also find it's the easiest thing to do because if you deal with two, three, or four people, you'll always need to sit down and discuss who gets what, how to let a partner out, and so on. You'll waste a lot of time—time better spent looking at properties, not babysitting people and their interests.

Limited Partnerships

Realize that partnerships, like snowflakes, are never alike. The easiest way to keep partnerships straight is to have them limited. I'm not necessarily, however, referring to the corporate structure called the limited partnership because limited in the legal sense means "limited to what a partner can lose." Rather, I'm referring to limited in the sense of time—six months, a year, three years, and so on—or simply limited to one specific deal.

It's easy to sit down with investors and ask, "What do you want to do?" Concern yourself with how they're putting money into the partnership, how they're receiving money over the course of the partnership, and when and how they'll get their money out. The last factor is usually the biggest concern because some people want their money all of a sudden for a specific reason. I suggest you define up front how your partners can get their money out and the time frame required from the time they tell you they need the money until the time you can deliver the funds.

When limiting a partnership agreement to a finite time frame, it's best to have a contract stating that the partnership will dissolve in one year from the date of that contract (or whatever time frame you agree on). Then if the partners are getting along, they can let that time frame pass, and the partnership is dissolved without hassle or arguments.

A partnership could also be limited to one deal and would need to be renegotiated for each deal thereafter. You don't necessarily need an attorney to set up a limited partnership unless your attorney advises you to do so. Remember, a limited partnership in the legal sense is a specific form of corporation. You might be able to get the same results by writing an agreement you've negotiated and then having an attorney review your document to make sure it's legally binding.

Three Kinds of Partnerships

You could form partnerships with investors in three ways:

1. Percentage: an investing partner gets a flat percentage interest rate
2. Equity: an investing partner takes risk with the investment to get a higher return
3. Combo: an investing partner gets a guaranteed return plus a portion of the equity

When you pay an investor a flat percentage interest rate, that person gets none of the appreciation in real estate or any cash flow in excess of the percentage interest rate. For example, if you guarantee an investor an 8 percent return, that's the amount of return received—even if the property doubles in value. This arrangement is typically accepted by someone who is averse to taking risks.

Setting up an equity arrangement with an investor implies he or she is willing to take risks with the investment to get a higher return. Mainly, the risk is that the deal doesn't go well and the investor loses money. Conversely, if the deal goes well, the investor makes a lot of money.

The combo investor wants a guaranteed return and a portion of the equity if the deal goes well. This kind of partner wants the best of both worlds. Wouldn't we all! There's nothing wrong with the concept, but such investors don't usually get as high a return as the other two types of investors.

PAYING INVESTORS

How do you know how much you can pay an investor? It's based on your cash flow, which is determined by doing a cash flow analysis.

For example, if you ask for $100,000 and your analysis tells you that your cash flow peaks at $10,000, you can't offer $12,000. Do you see the importance of coming up with all three scenarios of what you can pay an investor (percentage, equity, and combo) for each deal and then choose the one you want? It's important to understand what all the scenarios are, because people want different things. Be prepared to handle their requests in ways that create a win-win situation.

Making the Numbers Work

Once you've analyzed a deal, you want to see what and how you can realistically pay a partner. That might affect what type of partner you'll look for in putting a particular deal together.

Say you've determined you could offer a percentage partner 12 percent a year as a flat percentage. That means if the investor contributed $100,000, he would see a return of $12,000.

The equity investor gets a percentage of the property's value, which can be a high or low number depending on many factors. Let's say you've agreed to give this investor 50 percent of the deal, 50 percent of the cash flow, and 50 percent of the property appreciation. That means he or she also absorbs 50 percent of any potential losses. Remember, all of these numbers are net (after expenses), not gross.

The combo investor gets a combination of the other two. He or she receives a flat percentage return on the money invested, but it will typically be less than what you offer the percentage investor because of the equity portion of the agreement. In this example, the combo partner gets 8 percent and the percentage investor 12 percent. Similarly, this combo partner agreed to receive some equity but won't be offered as much as the equity-only investor. I call this smaller amount an equity kicker. In this example, let's say the equity kicker is 10 percent, not the 50 percent offered to the equity-only investor.

Percentage Partnership

How does a percentage partnership work? When you analyze a deal through REAPAC™, you'll realize what your potential cash flow is, and that becomes the maximum you can pay a partner. For example, if your partner invests $100,000 and your cash flow is $10,000 a year, the maximum you can pay is $10,000, or 10 percent. Therefore, you'd make that your ceiling and negotiate.

You'll be expected to match the common percentage payouts of whatever investment the partners are currently in. For example, if they're in the stock market, they'll expect a return of about 6 percent, which is typical of stock market returns over the last few years. Because your maximum amount to pay out in this example is 10 percent, it makes sense to look for people who have their money sitting in the bank in CDs earning 2 percent interest. If you offer 4 percent, they've just doubled their money, plus they now have a collatcralizcd investment. However, investment partners doing interest-only deals, or percentage partners, want a return of 8 to 10 percent, generally speaking.

When a person demands a guaranteed return from the deal, he's typically avcrsc to holding risk. In addition, a person who's looking to earn a flat return wants to "beat" a fixed rate of return he or she currently receives, such as through a certificate of deposit. I suggest that when you decide what percentage of interest partners should receive, start with the rates that CDs are paying.

To find out how to become an investor and how I set up my partnerships, go to http://www.LargeRealEstate.com and click on *investments*.

Proving the Numbers

For determining *exactly* what to pay, I have to prove the numbers to myself—just the way I determine market rents by placing ads in the paper at various rental rates. Here's how I do it.

Most people start investing at CD rates and work their way up. If CDs are now paying 2 percent, place an ad in the paper saying you'll pay more than 2 percent. Say you've placed an ad at 5 percent and have gotten no response. Next, place an ad for 6 percent. If there is still no response, place an ad for 7 percent, and on up.

P *l a c e   a n* A *d* O *f f e r i n g   14* P *e r c e n t*

If you want to attract partners willing to take a 7 percent return, place an ad like this: "Investor needed for $1 million, 14 percent return, collateralized on real estate."

Let's dissect that ad. The million dollars is the amount of money you want the investor to put up (a number that will vary with every deal). The 14 percent is the amount of money you're willing to pay a year (in this case, you'd pay $140,000 on $1 million). The ad tells the investor it's a collateralized loan, meaning there's "something" behind the investment to guarantee the investor's money, and you're telling the investor that the "something" (for example, an apartment building) is a piece of real estate.

Why would you state a 14 percent return when you know the average person would willingly accept 10 percent? First of all, when you analyze the deal, make sure your analysis shows you can actually pay that 14 percent return. And, of course, be willing to pay that amount to get the deal completed. When people call, explain the details of the deal and offer to send information on the property. (Be sure to do so after your nondisclosure, noncircumvention agreement has been signed.) Tell the people that it's a bidding process, and you'll make your decision in a week or so.

When you get another call on that ad, explain the deal again. Let's say the caller likes this deal and agrees to do it at 14 percent. Tell that person that another investor is also willing to do the deal at 14 percent. Chances are, you'll hear an offer of 13.75 percent. Tell that caller you'll decide in a week and a half whom you'll select to complete the deal with.

In the same vein, a third caller might offer 13.5 percent. You see that this process goes on until it gets to a point where these potential investors aren't willing to bid a lower percentage amount. The one who bids the lowest is the one you select as a partner.

To close the loop, contact all the previous potential investors and let them know what the winning offer was. When you do that, one of them might offer yet a lower interest rate.

It's wise to keep their phone numbers and addresses on hand. After all, you've spent time building rapport with them and have learned about their investing criteria. You've just built a database. They could be future partners.

Equity Owner

Equity owners are typically willing to take on risk when making a deal. Indeed, they need to, because they're looking to make a windfall profit if the property dramatically increases in value. When it comes to equity partnerships, people usually talk about a 50/50 split. But that needn't be true for every situation. I've seen new investors get anxious and maybe even greedy. They attempt to keep as much of the deal to themselves as possible. I see nothing wrong with making your fair share, but don't set yourself up for problems if you don't have the cash to handle them.

The Upside of a Deal

As long as you know you can handle the downside of a deal, then do the deal. Never worry about the upside (the amount of money you'll make) because if you've done your analysis correctly and meticulously selected your partners, then the upside takes care of itself. Money comes to you as a result of doing your homework. Just make sure that one potentially bad deal doesn't come back to bite you and stop you from doing other deals.

Can You Afford to Be Greedy?

Here's a critical lesson I learned about not keeping a high percentage of the ownership myself.

When I was putting together my first $4.25 million deal as a new investor, I wanted to keep half, if not more, of the deal as an equity investor. Other investors were willing to go in with me because it was such a strong deal. But my father asked me this: "You're going to be a 50/50 partner in this deal. That means you'll get 50 percent of the profits. What happens if there's a million-dollar problem with the building?" I had contractors look at it and made sure it would be rehabbed before I bought it; therefore, I didn't think it would present a problem. But for fun, I played along with my father's question. I couldn't see what he was getting at. He continued, "If there's a million-dollar problem with the building and you're a 50 percent owner, you'll have to come up with $500,000 to fix the problem. Do you have that much cash to put into the deal?"

This question brought reality home to me. I realized that the most important thing for me wasn't making a killing off that deal but getting it done and building a track record. At that point, even though putting the deal together was the most important aspect of the deal so far, I saw that *living through* the deal was actually more important. So I dropped the greed factor and was willing to take a smaller ownership of that property to gain valuable experience.

My advice: Keep my father's question in mind on every deal you do.

Luckily for me, that bad deal hasn't occurred in my investing career. Because of that, I've come up with what I consider the ideal approach, especially when it comes to equity partnerships.

Stair-Step Approach

I call this ideal the "stair-step" approach. (It can be applied to any of the three types of partnerships, but it applies most aptly to equity partnerships.) Here's how it works: If you're putting in your knowledge and an investor is putting in cash, to make the deal more interesting for the investor structure it at 90/10—that is, 90 percent in the investor's favor and 10 percent in your favor. That means you'll get 10 percent of the cash flow on the property and your partner gets 90 percent.

In your agreement, arrange for two things: First, as the cash investor gets his original investment paid back, his percentage of ownership decreases. Second, you can take some of your cash flow and keep it in the business by funneling it as a payment to the cash investor. Stipulate that you want to buy your way up to 51 percent ownership of the property. Once that investor gets his original cash investment back, he drops to 49 percent ownership or less, and you rise to 51 percent ownership or more—whatever amount you decide and write into the contract.

This approach allows you to accomplish a few things at once. First, you make the deal more interesting to the cash investor because he gets a larger ownership of the building and cash flow. Next, you show the investor your motivation to return his or her original investment. Third, you give yourself the ability to buy into a producing asset. As you run the property and see how well it's producing an income, you become more confident with the deal as it proves to be profitable under your watch.

This approach decreases your risk compared with beginning the deal with more than 50 percent ownership. Here's how: If you first buy the building as a 10 percent owner and you have a million-dollar problem right off the bat, you're only liable for $100,000 to fix it whereas your cash investor is liable for $900,000 (90 percent of the total). So if there's an immediate problem with the property, you don't have to come up with a lot of money. Over time, the investor gets more of his or her money back and the investor's percentage of ownership decreases. All the while, the likelihood of any unexpected problem with the property decreases. As time goes on, you're realizing more and more profit from the deal.

Combo Partner

Here's how a combo usually works. An investor comes in looking for a percentage return and says, "All I want is my 10 percent." Investors who ask for only 10 percent have typically been beaten up in the stock market and probably switched to bonds. Then when bonds took a financial hit, someone talked them into buying a piece of real estate that didn't do well as an investment. In such cases, investors don't know what to try next, so they look for a safe return with little risk and no bother.

You recognize a particular investor's apathy, but you try too hard to convince him that your deal is good. In fact, you pump it up so much that he definitely wants a piece of the action in the form of equity. He wants a 10 percent guaranteed return and 50 percent of the equity, but you realistically can't do that. So you reduce it to 7.5 percent guaranteed return with a 10 percent equity kicker. (I like to use that term because it sounds as though I'm doing investors a favor. I usually start at 5 percent, then double it if I have to, ending at 10 percent.)

PAYING YOURSELF

You might be reading this book with the intent of becoming a full-time real estate investor but might not have enough money to leave your job right now. Remember, when you structure a deal, you put time and effort into it as you do a job. Therefore, you should get compensated for that effort through a structuring fee. You'd add that fee to the purchase price and fully disclose it to the

No Limit of Combinations

Once you understand the basics of this combo approach, you're limited only by your creativity. You can structure these deals many different ways. For example: 8.5 percent for three years and then investors start getting their 10 percent equity, or 6.5 percent the first year, 7.5 percent the second year, 8.5 percent the third year, and the 10 percent equity kicks in the fourth year.

I usually offer a step-up like this: "I'll give you 7.5 percent now, 12 percent next year, and then 15.5 percent the third year." Two years are guaranteed. But I never pay higher than 15.5 percent because by the third year I'm already looking to refinance the property.

cash investor. It's commonly handled this way so you receive compensation for putting the deal together.

In addition, even though you will hire a management company to take care of the building, someone needs to watch over the management company and the corporation. You can do that for a salary, which is included as an expense in running the building. One word of advice: make that salary competitive. Don't overcharge a cash investor who's willing to do deals with you. Not that you shouldn't be paid handsomely and appropriately, but make sure it's in the realm of reality and fully disclosed.

USE PARTNERS ALL THE TIME

I started this chapter by asking you when you should use partners, and I leave you with this answer: use them all the time. Why? Say you bring an investment partner into a deal. Between cash flow and appreciation on the building, that investor makes 20 percent a year. Most likely, that person feels satisfied with you and will want to do more partnership investments. In this way, you're helping to secure your real estate future.

I show partners good money and make them very wealthy, especially the ones who think the way I do that building long-term wealth is important; that's a win-win.

If you've followed the guidelines I've set, there's a good chance your investment partners will brag to their friends about what they're doing with you. Most likely those friends will want to get involved. Again, you only want to deal with one entity so they would form a partnership. And because that one entity has more money to invest than a single individual would, you can do larger and larger deals. That's the logic of it.

In another example, let's say you have $100,000 to invest in a piece of property. On that property, between cash flow and appreciation you'll make $40,000 a year.

Now, I'm sure you'd be excited about making a 40 percent return on your money, especially as your money only makes $2,000—or a 2 percent return—sitting in the bank, right? But as a professional real estate developer, I can tell you that a 40 percent return wouldn't even get me out of bed in the morning. Here's why: If you structure that deal and bring in a cash investor who puts up $100,000 and you're going to split the profits 50/50, that means your investor will get $20,000, which is a 20 percent annualized return. But here's why you shouldn't be satisfied.

Say you structured this deal, got the financing, received compensation up front for putting the deal together, and are collecting a salary for running the building. That's icing on the cake. But splitting profits with that cash investor—well, that's the *real* cake. It means you equally split the $40,000, giving each of you $20,000. In this situation, the investor made $20,000 on $100,000 (a 20 percent return) and you made $20,000 without investing any money of your own. Therefore, a 40 percent return can't even be calculated, because you put no funds into the deal in the first place. In reality, your return can be infinite.

9

WORKING WITH A TEAM

When it comes to team building, I've learned that it's best to use the combined talents of your team members to accomplish one task rather than delegating one task to each person.

Here's what I mean. Say your team has ten members and you have ten tasks to complete. It would make sense for each team member to take charge of one task. Indeed, the average business owner thinks *this* is teamwork. This comes from specialization—the notion that each team member is expert at one thing and is only used for that one thing. That *sounds* logical, but it's not.

When I have a ten-member diversified team working on a project, I ask the team to tackle each task together. Why? To build cohesiveness and efficiency.

Here's an example. Say there are two experts on your team—one in sales and the other in property analysis—and you have a sales-related task that needs to get done. Whom would you assign that task to? Well, if you're an average business owner, you'd go right to your salesperson and say, "Will you handle this sales issue, please?"

My approach is different. I'd put the property analyst on the case, too, to bring in a different perspective and give pointers that will help the salesperson put together a stronger deal. For example, say the analyst spots a vital number in the preliminary calculations and wonders about it. The analyst tells the salesperson, who then puts that vital number to use in the sales process. That's how two minds work together. Imagine how effective ten minds working together can be. Do you see how much better your business will be when all your team members work on a task together? Of course, you'll require an overseer (that's my job) to ferry projects along and to steer the team out of bogs now and then. But having all experts work together is *my* idea of teamwork.

Bike **R**acing

Part of my training to prepare for my first Iron Man Triathlon—a 2.4-mile swim, followed by a 112-mile bicycle ride, and ending with a 26.2-mile run—included a 100-mile bicycle race from midtown Manhattan to Long Island's farthest point east and back. I hadn't been competing in triathlons all that long, so I wasn't as equipped for this race as I wanted to be. But I did want to give it my best shot.

The night before the race, I went to the local bike store to prep my bike. I bought extra water bottles to put in the cages (bottle holders) that screw onto my bike frame. I also bought a Piggyback, a device that hooks on the seat post, to hold two additional water bottles. I clamped them onto the seat post. "My bike was ready, but was I?" I thought.

The next morning I got up with the sun (5:00 AM) and took half an hour to get to the race's starting line, which was about two miles from my apartment. I had five minutes to relax before the starting gun. That's when I learned that the race route went down 59th Street and over the Hudson River via the 59th Street bridge into Queens and then into Long Island.

The group of cyclists I started with that morning had gone about 500 yards down 59th Street when I hit a recessed manhole cover and took a jarring bounce. I recovered quickly and kept pedaling . . . until I heard people yelling at me. They shouted that my two water bottles had shot out of the Piggyback. A cyclist retrieved them and handed them to me, saying (in his Australian accent), "I see you've got one of those *spring-loaded* Piggybacks," referring to the cyclists' in-joke about the Piggybacks' reputation for firing off water bottles as if they were rockets.

Well, three miles later, I lost those spring-loaded bottles for good in a similar bounce. This meant my capacity for drinking was cut in half.

Goofing around with those water bottles slowed me down and most of the cyclists had sprinted ahead of me. I had relied on them to show me the way because I couldn't decipher from the map where to go. Fear about getting lost started to set in. But I rode on and soon caught up to four cyclists who'd stopped to change a flat tire. I lent them a hand and then joined their group as we attacked the race together.

We immediately started to "draft," a bike-racing activity in which the cyclists form a line in single file to conserve energy. Moving at a fast pace, the leader takes the brunt of the wind and the cyclists behind clip along under his reduced resistance. Though the leader gets tired from dealing with the wind, he only has to stay in this front position five to ten minutes. When his time's up, he pulls to the left, slows down, allows the group to pass, pulls in to the back of the line, and recovers his energy while drafting off the cyclists in front of him. A fresh rider then leads the pack for a while.

When it comes to teams, it's good to understand how everyone contributes, determine the strengths and weaknesses of each team member, and benefit from working together. A cyclist riding alone usually averages 22 miles per hour; drafting cyclists can average 30 miles per hour, which is 33 percent faster. Which way would you want to try to win a race?

Continued

This race was set up in stages, with some stages starting closer to the finish line than others. I figured I'd stick with my group until I got to the next stage, where cyclists with fresh legs and more energy than I had were just starting to race.

When my group of five approached the fresh group of riders 25 miles later, I jumped into the new group. If riders from my former group wanted to join me, I welcomed them, but if they didn't, so be it. My objective was to not only finish the race but to finish it as quickly as possible.

In this manner, I hopped from group to group for the remainder of the race, slowing down only to drink water. As we got close to the end, a lot of cyclists began losing energy. A few others and I ended up as lone wolves, who grudgingly formed a lone wolf pack. Every one of us wanted to win.

Toward the end of the race, the course became hilly, and I got dizzy but was determined to finish anyway. There was no way to tell where I ranked in the race then (as it is in life), but I pedaled as if I were holding on to first place. As the race played out, I finished 12th out of 700 racers.

I knew a lot of people who were in much better shape than I was but didn't finish. I attribute my strong finish to my strategy of teaming up with fresh riders. I couldn't have finished 12th on my own. I know that.

It comes down to the fact that teams are more effective than individuals for accomplishing goals. Looking back, I'd have to say that all the teams (the groups I rode with) finished 12th too.

WINNING THE RACE WITH A MANAGEMENT COMPANY

The most important team member in the real estate business is glaringly obvious. Strong real estate businesses need good management companies on their teams. Why? Because real estate investors should be actively buying properties and growing their businesses, not dealing with day-to-day management issues.

However, investors often create their own management company to handle all aspects (acquisition through liquidation) of their business through their employees. Once they get a handle on managing their own properties, they think, "I can bring in *even more money* by managing other people's properties too."

In the beginning, when you first select the management company you want to work with, you behave more like a member of the management company's team than like a member of your *own* team. In that sense, it's common for new real estate investors to "draft" behind a management company that's been formed around an already successful real estate investor. In fact, I wouldn't have it any other way. I look for an experienced owner as an important criterion for picking a management company.

Typically, investors hire someone to run their property operations in addition to hiring superintendents, superintendents' assistants, construction workers, and contractors. For example, they'll either hire a broker or pay an employee to get a broker's license as a way to reduce acquisition costs. Then they hire a number of administrative assistants to help with all the paperwork. They'll likely also bring together outside team members such as lawyers and CPAs to help with legal and accounting work.

Opportunity Comes from Teamwork

Shrewd investors know that managing properties for other investors opens up opportunities for acquiring the buildings they manage in case they ever go up for sale. My cycling story reflects this: When I started the race all by myself and fumbled around with my water bottles, I was left in the dust. Investors who buy apartment buildings and try to manage them directly themselves do much the same thing. When I realized it was a mistake to go it alone in the race, I quickly got into gear and attached myself to a group (team)—the one on the side of the road ready to go. Sure enough, my speedometer registered 31 miles an hour instead of the 12 it was clocking earlier. I realized that bicycling teamwork can take me places fast, just as property management teamwork can too.

After you've accumulated a decent-sized total number of units (around 500 to 1,000), it makes financial sense to structure your own property management company to cut down on total management costs. Streamline it to reflect your own investment style.

ADDING AND FIRING TEAM MEMBERS

Right now, it probably seems that acquiring property is the hardest part about investing in real estate. I fully acknowledge that. But I have to tell you, I think the process of adding team members is also hard, and having to leave team members—or, worse yet, fire them—is hardest of all. It's tough, but that's business. Strong business owners—like strong cyclists—can't win if they stick with weak team members.

There are differing opinions about this team-building approach, so make your own choices. I'm supportive of all of my team members and work with them as much as possible and as long as possible. I balance that well, but in the long run I believe in winning the race, so I'm conscious of selecting the best team members I can.

Filling Team Positions

The management company, as I said, is your first and most important team member. Use that resource to its fullest, as I did with my cycling team.

After the management company, your next team member is a tax attorney. Just as you would at the beginning of any new venture, you want to keep costs as low as possible while still making the venture viable. Tax attorneys accomplish this because they deal with both law *and* accounting. (Eventually, you'll hire both an attorney and an accountant, but for the time being I suggest you use a "jack-of-two-trades.")

Here are some general interview questions I ask whenever I'm filling the position for a tax attorney on my team. Indeed, these questions apply to anyone I might bring on my team.

1. Do you have clients who are real estate investors? Specifically, are they investors who buy 50-unit or fewer unit apartments? There's a big difference between 50-unit buildings and larger ones. For example, a building that has 50 units requires much less maintenance, less engineering, and less construction than does a 100-unit building, not only based on size but on complexity. Almost any construction company can work on smaller buildings; for a construction company, working on a 40-unit building is little different from working on a 20-unit building.

A bigger building just plain has more mass and surface area to deal with. With a complex physical structure, there's more wear and tear, more elevators requiring stronger support, more extensive safety codes, and more trash management systems (for example, a 20-unit building might have four garbage bins, whereas a 100-unit building has a trash chute and possibly an incinerator). Given these big differences, look for team members whose clients handle the same types and sizes of buildings as you do.

2. Do you personally have any real estate experience? Have you purchased any of your own properties? I'm not looking for full-time real estate investors as much as I'm looking for team members who have gone through acquisition/liquidation phases of real estate investment. If potential members say, "I built my own home; I bought a fixer-upper and own a fourplex that I manage myself—all in the time frame of about five years," that's fine with me. I just want to know that they've had a taste of what I do.

3. What references do you have? I talk to attorneys' clients to find out exactly what these attorneys do for them. I also want to know if these clients are satisfied with the attorneys' performance. I always try to accomplish more than one thing at a time—and when hiring a new attorney, I'm also prospecting. If I hire tax attorneys whose clients do what I do, I know those attorneys will be a great resource for me. When I contact clients, I ask myself, "Can this person potentially be a cash investor with me? Can this client bring business to me too?"

I don't have to hire a particular tax attorney to get in touch with his or her clients later so long as I've received permission. In fact, I let the attorney decide *how* I should make contact. I certainly don't want to develop a bad reputation or burn bridges by mishandling these connections.

PICKING MORE TEAM MEMBERS

Now that you have selected a tax attorney, you'll most likely want to add other members to your team. Remember, your team will be built not only on the services you need but also on your successes. Note: Some team members will be independent contractors rather than employees.

Here's a quick overview of possible team members you'll want to have:

- Management company
- **Tax attorney/CPA**—accounting, legal documents, evictions
- Attorney
- CPA
- **Title company rep**—closings
- Real estate brokers (licensed and aggressive)—property acquisitions
- Brokers' assistants
- **Lenders or mortgage brokers** (Remember, cash is king.)
- Operations manager
- Superintendents

- Administrative assistants
- **General contractors**—building/apartment rehabs
- Construction workers
- Building inspectors

For more information on my team members, visit http://www .LargeRealEstate.com and click on *team members.*

W *h a t* **D** *o e s* **A** *g g r e s s i v e* **M** *e a n ?*

Everyone seems to define the word *aggressive* differently. Here's my definition: a quick answer followed by substantiating proof when I ask brokers a question about a property. For example, if I ask what average market rents are in an area and they tell me "other clients are doing well," that's not an answer. (At best, that's politics. And who are most famous for skirting a question with a nonanswer? Politicians.) I prefer to hear a number like $500 a month, followed by substantiating proof such as rent rolls from those rentals. Another answer I'll accept is this: "I don't know, but let me find that out." I'd much rather have an "I don't know" than a guess. After all, real estate brokers earn commissions; and a 6 percent commission on a $3,000,000 building is $180,000, which certainly is good money. For that amount of money, I expect all my questions answered to my satisfaction.

FINISHING THE RACE STRONG

Management teams rely on their leaders. Your team will be relying on you and so will your tenants and prospective tenants. Once you have a team together and you're working well, go out and *take* the lead.

In my Long Island training bike race, I finished in 12th place because of the cyclists I rode with along the way. Doing so meant

I had enough energy and resources to finish the race in as high a place as possible. Because I had worked I was probably the most tired of them all, but it was worth it! That's why I can say, "All my teams finished 12th." This is true for you too. Use all of your team members to help you succeed.

In what position will your team "finish" the race you're in?

For more information, visit http://www.LargeRealEstate.com and click on *team members.*

CLOSING ON THE PROPERTY

I think of closing as being akin to taking flight lessons. About halfway through the process to get a pilot's license, a student is required to fly solo, which means taking a plane up and landing it three times with no assistance.

When I did my first solo flight, my safety net—my flying instructor, Todd—wasn't sitting beside me. I had been working on Wall Street in the day and taking lessons at night at the Morristown, New Jersey airport. Todd told me I had to come back in the daytime to solo so I could get my VFR rating (Visual Flight Rating as compared with IFR, Instrument Flight Rating). But after a nighttime lesson, he said, "I think you're ready to solo." So we landed the plane and did a quick check, and then Todd said, "I want you to take off and land three times."

Todd walked over to the control tower and informed the air traffic controller I would be soloing. The controller gave me clearance to take off. I taxied out on the runway, gave it full throttle, took my foot off the brakes, and started racing down the runway. At 60 miles an hour, I pulled on the controls and lifted the nose into the air. I took off feeling confident—until I reached an altitude of 1,400 feet. That's when I had to turn the plane and begin my three touch-and-go landings.

At this point, reality set in.

Until then, I'd flown fearlessly for 12 to 15 hours and made 10 to 15 landings with Todd. In the back of my mind, I knew he could make adjustments if I did something wrong. But being on my own changed everything. I almost panicked as I repeatedly asked myself, "How will I get this plane on the ground?" When I talked to the air traffic controller, I didn't want my nervousness to come across in my voice, but inside my head the doubts raced around like hamsters in a cage. "How was I going to get this plane on the ground? Maybe I could keep flying around until it ran out of fuel. Yeah, but if I did, it would crash. I'd be better off trying to land this thing after all. If a crash happens, it happens."

As these thoughts raced through my mind, amazingly my training intuitively kicked in. Even though I was nervous, my mind kept me busy with fears of crashing, while my body was going through the necessary steps to land. Before I knew it, I was 30 feet off the ground in perfect position. I did a perfect flare, which means I kept the nose wheel slightly off the ground while letting the main wheels touch the pavement effortlessly for a smooth landing.

Then, just when I'd recovered my confidence, three deer ran in front of the plane. Again, my training kicked in. I remained calm, contacted the tower, and notified the controller about the deer on the runway.

Then I hit full throttle and took off again, leaving the security staff to handle the deer. From that point on, I remained calm and highly focused. That's when flying solo became fun. I did it! I had accomplished the first touch-and-go and came around for the second one. And as I went up for my third, my confidence soared.

Your First Closing

Just like going solo ends the process of learning to fly, so does the closing appointment end a stage of learning in real estate.

The first real estate closing I did felt like my solo flight in the airplane—with lots of fear mixed in. But because I had the right training and the right team members, I was able to complete the process and purchase the property.

Your first closing—your first solo—will be the scariest, most nerve-racking time for you. You might even "see deer on the runway" at that closing! Just remember that every time you "land," doing it becomes easier and more fun. And have faith that, at the necessary point, your training will kick in to help you accomplish your goal.

BEING PREPARED FOR THE CLOSING

Before giving you a specific strategy for closing, I want to explain the theory behind it and why you need it by describing what often happens at the meeting when people close on a deal.

One of the biggest mistakes I see not only from beginners but also from professionals in real estate is not being prepared for the closing. Both groups believe that the contract and all the negotiations up to this point will save them from any hassles or eleventh-hour negotiations. They hope everything will go well, but hope is usually a byproduct of fear. In other words, to balance feeling fearful, people *hope* events will happen a certain way.

I suggest that instead of hoping, focus on *taking action*. If you wait until the last day of your contract to close on a property, you leave yourself with no room to maneuver. You can get backed against the wall and lose the time, effort, and money that you've put into this deal. Believe me, people on the other side of the table could take advantage of this situation. Two people who come to mind are the seller and the lender. The seller, knowing that you've run out of time, will sometimes ask for a higher purchase price or other contingencies. The lender might say, "We realize that this is a riskier situation than we first thought, so therefore we have to charge more points or a higher interest rate." (Note: one point is 1 percent of the amount of money borrowed.)

By not planning ahead, you've opened yourself up for financial abuse. However, if you do what I outline here (and follow what's in Chapter 7 under contracts and addenda), you won't face these problems.

ANATOMY OF A DEAL

The owners of a 16-unit apartment building in West Harlem, New York, wanted $1 million for selling it. One of my brokers, Scott, introduced the deal to me because it fit my criteria for deals I like to do.

The owners already had an offer on the property for $950,000 cash, but that didn't faze me, because one of the things I'm good at is creative financing. After receiving the property setup sheet on this building, I ran the numbers and saw that it already enjoyed good cash flow. And it projected excellent potential cash flow if I rehabbed the building.

I addressed Scott: "It looks like a good building, so why are they selling it?" He said three partners owned it and had a falling out. He had mentioned my interest in the deal to one of the partners and explained I had a strong reputation as an experienced investor. That partner was interested in my participation. Recently bitten by the real estate bug, he wanted to learn the ropes of investing by working with me.

With that information in hand, I thought, "If he wants to work with me, he'll have to make some concessions, and he'll need to have some exchange in this partnership." I found a way I could structure this deal and actually pay more than the asking price of

$1 million, creating a win-win situation for everyone. I decided to offer $1.2 million.

Here's how it worked. From my cash flow analysis, I saw I could get financing for $800,000. Because my purchase offer was $1.2 million (by no coincidence), each partner would get $400,000 cash. Therefore, the two partners leaving the deal would get $800,000 and my potential protégé would take his $400,000 in the form of a note payable over the next ten years. His first payment would start no sooner than one year (12 months) after closing. Also, for the first three years, he would receive only 50 percent of the amortized monthly payment from the cash flow of the building, or $1,200 a month. From years four through six, he would receive 75 percent of the amortized monthly payment, or $1,800 a month. From years seven through ten, he would receive the full amortized payment of $2,400 a month. At the end of the tenth year, he'd receive a balloon payment for the remaining amount.

This deal allowed him and his partners to receive more than their asking price. He would get his share with interest, which, within this payment structure, resulted in a large cash flow. He would also stay on as partner and receive the ownership benefits of tax write-offs and appreciation.

Everyone involved thought this idea set up a win-win situation. After all, how many sellers get a higher offer on a property than the amount they ask?

However, as fate took its course, this deal couldn't be completed because one of the partners already had an agreement with the initial cash buyer. He'd accepted the offer of the $950,000 cash, and because it was under contract, this agreement couldn't be broken. Generally, when a deal doesn't go through, I simply say "next" and move on.

About two months later, I was talking to Scott and asked, "Whatever happened with that building in West Harlem? Did the deal go through?"

"It's funny you should ask," he said and went on to explain that the buyer was doing a 1031 tax-deferred exchange. A 1031 exchange relates to a tax law—Internal Revenue Code 1031— stating that when someone sells a building and purchases another building, he or she can avoid paying capital gains tax on the proceeds as long as the acquired property is of "like or greater value." This law requires owners to locate an exchange property within 45 days and close on it within six months. When you deal with big properties, six months is a short time. That's why seller financing works so well. Sellers regard 1031 exchanges (also known as like-kind exchanges) as a good way to get interest-free money without tax consequences.

After the cash buyer put down $250,000 on the building, he was having trouble getting financing for the remainder. I told Scott, "Have the buyer give me a call. Maybe there's something I can do." When this buyer called, I told him I could get the money for the balance by structuring a partnership agreement. In that agreement, we'd each come away with 50 percent ownership, and I'd have 51 percent day-to-day control of the building.

Remember, this buyer was facing the possibility of losing $250,000 in cash in less than two weeks. I knew the sellers liked my offer, but I also knew that they were looking at $250,000 in cash that couldn't be refunded. This buyer clearly wasn't in a good position, but still greed kicked in. As soon as I asked for a partnership arrangement, he downplayed his struggles and backed off. He said he'd think about it, but he never got in touch with me again.

Think about this. Several lenders had already told him they wouldn't lend him money, but he was willing to lose that money rather than make less than he'd originally planned.

Now I knew the exact closing date of this deal, so I got in touch with Scott the night of the scheduled closing to find out what had happened. He said, "I've never seen anything like this before. The lenders knew it was the last day he could close on the deal. They were going to charge him three points on his borrowed money. Then they squeezed him for another six points, making a total of nine points, and raised the interest rate 2.5 percent. With all other costs involved, in order to close on that building, he had to come up with another $90,000 in cash—not to mention the added monthly payments on his borrowed funds.

"Because he'd been too busy trying to get his financing, he failed to get the paperwork to the title company ahead of time. It gave the lenders an opportunity to reassess the paperwork at closing and raise the dollar amounts. They told him, 'You didn't reveal certain items earlier and if we had known, we would have given you different numbers.' He had no legal recourse because he'd sent over his paperwork late."

The deal is never over until the fat banker sings.

This story clearly indicates the importance of completing the paperwork 72 hours before the closing date. Make sure the lender and the title company have it in plenty of time to see if they have any objections before closing. Submitting the paperwork well beforehand allows everyone involved to adjust if necessary. So if the lender had tried to make a change at closing, the buyer could lose his deposit but would still be able to sue the lender for damages, arguing that the lender had ample opportunity to review it.

In fact, we feel so strongly about demanding paperwork ahead of time that in my company, we spell that out through an addendum to the contract and always include it. Because of this clause, if the paperwork doesn't arrive for whatever reason, I can cancel the closing if I choose. Of course, any expenses would have to be picked up by the sellers because their representatives created the delay.

Taking Care of Inspections

Somewhere between the offer being accepted and the closing, you definitely want to inspect the building. Typically, I hire a contractor to inspect it with me so he can explain what needs to be done to improve the property and which repairs are most urgent. From there, if any work needs to be done, I require three estimates from contractors and compare the estimates.

When you go through the inspection process, be most concerned with these three major areas: roof, boilers, and windows. By fully examining the roof, boilers, and windows, you can get a general feel of the condition of the property as a whole.

CLOSING IN A SPEEDY, EFFICIENT WAY

In my opinion, the definition of professionalism requires that transactions are set up in a speedy and efficient manner, which means coordinating with others who are willing to work at your desired pace. To gain efficiency, I always turn to my key teammate, the property management company. Read on to understand what you need to know about the closing so you can have your management company take you through it.

As noted earlier, the first thing is making sure you receive all the paperwork (see list that follows) required 72 hours before the closing date. (I suggest you state in your contract that the closing will take place 72 hours after receipt of the paperwork. This means that if the paperwork arrives on the day of the closing, the closing itself would automatically get delayed 72 hours.) Take time to review this paperwork, making sure everything is in order and that it's all up to date.

Paperwork Required

The following lists the paperwork needed for the closing. Because each transaction is different, this isn't an all-inclusive list. Rather, use it as a guideline to help you understand what to look for at closing. Also consult with your property management company about what's needed for a specific closing.

The seller needs to provide you with the following:

- A copy of the rent roll
- A copy of the collections report
- Detailed expense report (a list of expenses to look at is given in REAPAC™)
- A copy of all utility bills
- Copies of all work done on the property in the last three years and any warranties associated with that work
- Any and all escrow accounts (i.e., money put aside to pay taxes and other lump-sum payments)
- All rental deposits
- A copy of all financing on the property (i.e., existing debt service)
- Copies of all violations pertaining to the building
- Notice of any pending legal actions
- Copies of permits for work done and for work that needs to be done
- If applicable, all government documents (i.e., if the building you're buying houses Section 8 tenants)

Arrange for a final inspection, which is typically scheduled 24 to 48 hours before you plan the closing.

Close Early If You Can

Remember, although the contract may say you'll close 90 days from the signing of the contract, that doesn't mean that you need to wait until the 90th day to actually close. In fact, most of the time you want to close as soon as possible, because turning deals is how you make your living. The more transactions you complete, the more profits you bring in.

And keep in mind that you have a secret weapon that allows you to close early. Whereas the average investor usually has to wait for conventional financing to become available, your creative financing strategies allow you to finance deals more quickly and easily than the average investor. Most of the time, you'll use seller financing, which is a way to obtain cash more quickly. This will increase the number of transactions you handle, thus profits, as well.

Costs Involved in Closing

Some costs just can't be eliminated from the closing, but many of them are postponed until the closing and/or built into your financing. You can also have the seller split some of the costs or, in some cases, pay for all of them. In addition, if outside investors are involved, you can often build these closing costs into the amount of money they put up for the property. Be sure to tell them you're doing that.

Team Members at Closing

As I said before, one of your most important team members is the management company. I find that people working in most management companies are underused, but you can get them involved in property acquisition, property maintenance, rehab, property readiness for sale, and assistance in selling. They provide valuable services to you; make sure you're using their talents fully.

I emphasize this point because going through the closing process can be a scary experience in the beginning. However, you can remove the fear if you have your management company rep holding your hand, explaining everything you need in order to do a speedy, efficient job of closing on a property.

Can't a real estate broker help you with closing? A broker will tell you what you legally need to close on the property, but it's better to have someone involved who has a vested interest in this property. The management company rep not only knows what's needed to close but also what you need as the new owner of the building. If you work with the same management company as the previous owner did, you have an added advantage of already having the inside scoop. Bottom line: find a good management company.

I suggest that you attend your first few closings to understand the process inside and out. Your team members should include a real estate broker (if you used one), a title company representative, and someone from the property management company. Also consider having a tax attorney, depending on what's needed.

Attending your first closings is a great learning opportunity. However, over time it's sometimes not wise to be there. Now, *not* going to a closing might seem like a new concept, but sometimes, as outlined below, there's a good reason for it. If you choose not to go, be sure to go to your management company, title company, or attorney (whoever will be doing the closing on your behalf) and sign all of the paperwork either the day before or the morning of the closing. Then make yourself accessible by phone in case you run into any problems.

THE ART OF NEGOTIATION

On only rare occasions do I attend closings these days because of a specific strategy that I've implemented. The idea for it came from meeting Herb Cohen, who's written *You Can Negotiate Anything* and *Negotiate This!*–the two books I highly recommended earlier.

Herb told me to never negotiate unless the person who's authorized to make the decisions sits across the negotiating table from you. Otherwise you're wasting your time.

Herb also told me that to avoid getting backed into a corner, the decision maker on a deal (you) shouldn't go to the negotiation table. Instead, send team members, such as your lawyer and/or property management representative, to be your intermediaries at the actual closing.

I've learned from Herb Cohen and others that there's no one specific way to negotiate. All the time, you hear "never be the first one to talk." Let's face it; nothing would ever take place if both people read the same book and followed the same instructions. There's a time and place for everything.

I believe it's especially important to be flexible when it comes to negotiating. (I'd love to tell you that I've negotiated only one way for everything I've received, but that wouldn't be true.) I've learned ways to handle an adversary from the writings of the Kung Fu martial arts expert, Bruce Lee. He went against thousands of years of training when he declared that specific moves, used robotically, often don't work. Instead, it's best to improvise and adapt to every situation you meet. (I suggest reading any of Bruce Lee's writings on this topic.)

Remember, remain flexible in your negotiations and understand your options before you enter into negotiations.

A *Sporting* **C**ompetition

Another person who has strongly influenced me is chess grand master Bobby Fischer. I watched a video of Bobby playing chess with approximately 20 people at once. He'd walk up to a chess board, look at it for about five seconds, make his move, and walk over to the next table to play there. Coincidentally, he won all 20 matches.

Bobby wrote that whenever he goes into a chess tournament, he holds his opponent in contempt. Now, I don't think I hold sellers I work with in contempt. Nonetheless, Fischer did make me look at negotiating as a sporting competition. This approach has helped me, because coming from an athletic background, I know the preparation that goes into playing sports. Athletes spend four or five days preparing for one day, which equals 15 hours of preparation for 3 hours of competition. In addition, they spend the morning of the event getting psyched up, as well as getting adrenalin-pumping moments before the game.

That's the stance I take when negotiating. I say this not to be dramatic but to stress this point: When you go in to a closing to buy an apartment building, you're playing in the Super Bowl or the World Series.

MY STRATEGY FOR CLOSING

Because you've had the paperwork in hand for 72 hours, you and the members of your team have had time to become familiar with it. If everything checks out, I suggest you sign the paperwork the night before, or the morning of, the closing.

Even when you're not attending the closing, it's critical to make yourself accessible. I typically clear my schedule that day and wait by a phone to receive any calls from my team members at the table so I can handle any eleventh-hour situations.

Typically, one of my attorneys goes to the closing table. If there are any last-minute negotiations, such as the seller's trying to get more concessions or the lender's trying to get more money in the form of additional points or higher interest rates, I'm not there to accept their advances. So the seller has to negotiate with my attorney first, and he's not the final decision maker.

My Attorney Ricci

Ricci and his wife, Sandy, have been friends of mine for 16 years. Ricci and I attended Temple University together and then he went on to law school. At times, he speaks at my events and tells the class, "I'm a predator. I go around and look for assets. If your assets aren't protected, I'll go after them. I look for people whose wallets are fat and juicy so I can bite into their assets if they're hanging out there. If not, I'll move on and look for other assets."

Don't get me wrong. He's a great person, but he's also a great competitor. He's my first line of defense. My wish for you is to have your own Ricci on your team.

So if the seller or lender requests any changes at closing, he or she must first talk with one of my attorneys like Ricci. He initially might respond by saying, "I don't think my client will like this change, but I'm willing to hear what you have to say." The sellers spell out their new demands, and Ricci takes this opportunity to negotiate back and forth. Once he accomplishes as much as he thinks he can, he says, "I have to give my client a call, but I can tell you that he won't be happy about this change." Then he calls me and the conversation goes something like this:

"Hey, Greg, how are you?"

"Fine. How's the family?"

"Sandy and the kids are fine. We went to the Eagles game over the weekend," and so on.

Then I'll ask, "What's going on there?" He'll say, "Nothing. They just have a few questions." I'll respond, "Give me a call back if you need me."

Ricci goes back to the table and says, "I've never seen him so furious in my life! He's not sure we can continue with the closing under these new circumstances."

Ricci negotiates further and calls me again to convey what the new round of negotiations brought about. Ultimately, I do want this property to close on that day so I'm willing to negotiate. But see how the sellers were forced to negotiate with someone else first before they got to the ultimate decision maker? Do you see how that strategy plays out in my favor?

Remember, I strategically put clauses in my contract to extend the closing to another date if need be, so I don't paint myself into a corner. (See the contract section in Chapter 7 for wording.)

11

MANAGING THE BUILDING

You've been through quite a full process. Your offer was accepted. You've set a closing date on the property. The management company has taken you through the building, and you've received detailed expense reports. Your next step is to review all the paperwork needed for closing over the next 72 hours. You need to show up in person for the final inspection. If all goes well at closing, then the outcome you want—owning an apartment building—will be yours.

Most likely, your management company has been with you throughout this process. Going forward, it can assist you in many different ways: locating properties, understanding financing, staying with you through future closings, and, most probably, staying on board to manage your properties.

TIPS ON MANAGING THE MANAGEMENT COMPANY

How do you manage the management company? First, insist that it integrates with the procedures already in place. Have it use the same paperwork (for example, announcements, eviction notices, and update letters) written in the same format that the previous owner used. That way, tenants aren't alerted to a change in ownership. When they know a new owner has come in, some tenants test the waters and don't pay rent, figuring the new owner doesn't have the records and probably won't be diligent in chasing them down.

When renters don't pay, I suggest having your management company send missed payment notices three days in a row. Follow those with an eviction notice if necessary. This lets remiss renters know the new owner takes collecting rents seriously. You want the changeover to seem seamless to your tenants.

Legally, tenants have ten days to make their rent payments. That means if rent is due on the first, tenants have until the tenth of the month to pay. There's no benefit to starting an eviction procedure early. If you begin sending notices on the fifth for three days and a dispute over not paying the rent goes to housing court, the judge can throw out your case because you didn't give ten days' notice as required. Because of this timing, I recommend closing your purchase deal on the tenth of the month. This makes the previous owners or management company responsible for sending out eviction notices. It's bad public relations for the first communication from the new owner of the building to be an eviction notice.

Be sure to carefully manage the management company early on. It's your building and you need to know everything that affects it.

Marketing

I recommend putting up a sign or banner outside the building (such as a yellow sign made at a copy store stating "1, 2, 3 bedroom starting at $x") to entice people to stop in. There's nothing wrong with prospective tenants asking to rent a unit and being

Keep in Touch with the Operation of Your Property

Some real estate people I've met haven't been the brightest. For example, I met an investor in Oklahoma who bought a fully leased building. He turned it over to a management firm, then moved to Florida, and ignored the property for 18 months. Well, it wasn't long before the building's occupancy dropped to below 50 percent.

The owner faced lots of other problems too. The management company refused to do $150 worth of repairs to a unit so it could be rented. Consequently, the unit sat vacant for 12 months, and the owner lost $4,600 in rent. (Remember that real estate has a leverage factor of 1:10, so losing $4,600 in rent cost the owner $46,000 in property equity.) The management company also missed a mortgage payment, and the bank accelerated its debt service, which cost this owner a lot of money to get his *own* property out of foreclosure.

That's what can happen when you don't regularly keep in touch with the operation of your property. Remember, when you buy a property, you're buying the previous owner's profits *and* problems.

told, "There's no vacancy right now, but please leave your name and contact information. We'll put you on a waiting list." In fact, doing this is great PR. It builds the perception that your building is in high demand, thus making it seem even more desirable to prospects. The management company can let them know when units become vacant.

Also, constantly run a small ad in the paper. That way you'll keep your building full and stay at maximum rent. Some people forget they have to plan for the future; they start thinking about putting an ad in the newspaper at the point when they need tenants. Instead, place ads early to help you build a waiting list. You'll spend more on advertising, but you're better off in the long run by having a solid waiting list.

Let's face it, turnover happens before you know it. If you have 20 units and even have two-year leases, that means you should have a lease coming up every other month. You're always dealing with supply and demand in this business after all.

When tenants approach 90 days from the end of their lease, start contacting them, stating, "Your lease is coming due. Please let us know your plans so we can set up a new contract." Typically, they won't respond until the last 30 days.

INCREASING RENTS

There are two situations in which it's difficult to increase rents: One is a dilapidated building; the other is mishandling expiring leases. Here's what happens when management companies don't give advance notice of expiring leases. Within 14 days before a lease is due for renewal, a tenant comes in and asks to renew the lease, only to be told for the first time that the rent is going up. The tenant usually says, "Well, I thought my rent was going to stay the same. I didn't know it was going to increase. I might not renew my lease after all."

If you don't have prospective tenants lined up, most of the time the existing tenant negotiates to keep the rent at the existing rate and you'll feel obligated to accept. Why? Because if the tenant leaves, you will have to market the unit and risk having it vacant for a few weeks or more.

Let's say you intended to raise the rent $100 a month, from $1,000 to $1,100, which means that over a year, you'll collect an extra $1,200. But if that tenant moves out and the apartment sits vacant for four weeks, you've just lost $1,100 in rent. Raising the rent by $100 doesn't matter anymore; you've just lost that money in one month of vacancy. What's more, if you miss that one month's rent at $1,100, your property value has just dropped

$15,000 because you have costs in maintenance, insurance, and so on. That comes directly out of your pocket. Most large buildings can sustain a vacancy better than small ones can. Still, you can't afford to have too many vacancies in this business.

Do you see how landlords forfeit getting maximum rent? It's not that owners don't want to increase the rent; it's just that they don't communicate ahead of time. If, on the other hand, you've been constantly marketing and your tenants aren't sure they want to renew because of a rent increase, you can reply, "I fully understand. But you'll need to be out in two weeks because I have a waiting list. People want to move into that unit and are willing to pay the increased amount." Hearing that usually persuades them to accept the rent increase and gives you your maximum rent.

Always Market

Never stop marketing your units. Consistent marketing not only saves you money in the long run, but it can *make* you a lot of money by keeping your units occupied and allowing you to increase rents.

MANAGING BAD TENANT SITUATIONS

A lot of people stay out of real estate because they don't want to have to fix toilets at one o'clock in the morning. I don't want to fix toilets, even mine, at one o'clock in the morning either. But I do love having tenants.

A lot of worry associated with being a landlord is due to the fear of dealing with bad tenants. A bad tenant is someone who deliberately breaks that toilet! People also have visions of being raked over the coals by their tenants and consequently being caught in endless tenant housing disputes. This could very well happen but only if you, the owner, allow that to happen. If you don't exercise control and authority as an owner of a property, can you honestly expect the tenants to have much respect for you or the property? (Ethically they should and I understand that, but let's look at actual practice.) Would you allow someone to come into your house and break the kitchen sink? If not, then why would you allow that to happen in your property? Okay, you might unknowingly let a bad tenant in the door, but as long as you know how to handle that person, his or her bad behavior shouldn't spread to other tenants in the building.

Let me make a strong point about this. People believe that when they take over a building, they'll have to deal with a number of bad tenants—the type who sprays graffiti on a building or scratches names in the front window. Although it might seem there are a number of these people, the problem usually comes down to one person: the ringleader. If you can eradicate that person, the others will "cease and desist" their criminal behavior.

Who is this ringleader? It's the person who tells other tenants, "The owner of the building is a millionaire. It doesn't seem like he cares about the building. If I were you, I'd break the front window. That will show him." That's who you need to get rid of; the others are followers. Make sure tenants follow the right lead—yours.

Section 8 Tenants

If a problem arises in which a Section 8 tenant continues to skip paying rent or causes other problems, go directly to HUD with complete documentation and tell the representatives you've fixed what was broken in the apartment (and have photos to prove it), but the tenant still refuses to pay rent. Let the HUD representatives handle it.

J u s t **F** i x t h e **L** i g h t **S** w i t c h

As an example of a bad tenant, I had a nasty situation in the first apartment building I purchased. As is often the case, the management company and the bad tenant were facing off head to head. The tenant refused to pay rent because he claimed that his apartment needed repairs. He protested that he knew his tenants' rights; he didn't have to pay rent. The management representatives took the stand that it had had this problem with the same tenant even before I became the owner and had finally "had it" with this ringleader. Unfortunately, the management company had "had it" at my expense. When I looked at the management reports, I saw that this tenant hadn't paid rent in three months. The company reps responded by saying they had decided to handle this tenant dispute in court.

Now in New York especially, tenant disputes can become extremely messy for any building owner. Let's face it; some areas of the country are more tenant friendly than are others. Nonetheless, my experience tells me the old saying is still true: No one wins in a court of law. So I wanted to avoid taking that route.

This problem tenant was a Section 8 tenant who'd lived there a few years. He had taken advantage of the previous owners, who didn't want to draw attention to something they were doing by taking him to court.

To resolve the problem as the new owner, I tried to rationalize with reps from the management company, but logic and reason had long since been thrown out the window. So I turned to my mentor and explained that the tenant wouldn't pay rent because he said the light switch in the apartment was broken. With words of wisdom, my mentor simply said, "Fix the light switch."

"But you don't understand," I argued. He cut me off right there. I'm glad he did—I was just about to justify the management company's position as I'd found myself embroiled in its point of view too. He said, "I don't care what problems this tenant has created. Fix the light switch, *but do it right.*"

Continued

"What do you mean by that—do it right?"

"You want to create a paper trail," he advised, and he began to detail a strategy I've learned to use over the years. Based on his advice, here's what I did.

I instructed the management company reps to immediately inform the tenant that they were coming into the apartment to make repairs. It was obvious the tenant didn't want them to do the needed repairs so he wouldn't have to pay rent. Given that, of course he didn't return their phone calls. But local law requires that the landlord makes three attempts to fix the problem. (Every city and state has different regulations when it comes to tenant law, so first check with the housing board in your area about how to legally apply the following strategy.)

We sent the tenant three certified letters, each stating we needed to have access to the unit. We also made phone calls and slipped notes under the door of his apartment. After the third certified letter, we were then let into the unit to make the necessary repairs. For safety's sake, I had the management company send two workers (not one) for two reasons: (1) in case the tenant was present and felt agitated, and (2) one extra worker as a witness to ensure that the work was completed. While the workers were in the apartment, they took notes and photographs as they looked for other repairs that needed to be done. Then they contacted the management company, got approval to do the work they'd noted, and completed it. Before leaving, they took photographs to verify that the repairs had been finished.

What did they find? The workers discovered that the tenant had (as the management company guessed) taken a hammer to the light switch and broken it. As dramatic as that was, I wasn't concerned because it only cost a few bucks for a light switch versus more than $1,000 a month for rent. All totaled, the work in that unit came to $73 for materials and a bit more than $100 for labor. If the tenant broke anything after that point, the responsibility for repairs would lie with him, because having the photographs and other documentation protected us. As soon as the workers finished, my attorney then sent the tenant a letter demanding payment and a notice of possible eviction. At that point, the tenant realized how seriously we were handling this and decided it was best to move out. His departure resulted in considerably fewer problems in the building, as he had been the ringleader there.

Here's why I say that. HUD is really renting the apartment, and if you're not keeping the building up to standard, HUD can stop payment for that tenant (if not payments for all tenants) until the problem is fixed. If tenants are refusing to pay rent for no justifiable reason, HUD can throw them off the Section 8 assistance rolls permanently.

It all comes down to this: If you have a fear of getting into real estate and making a million dollars because tenants might call you about a broken toilet at one o'clock in the morning, in the wise words of my mentor, "Fix the toilet."

So that's how you manage the tenants. Don't wait for a problem to emerge in order to have face time with the tenants. Walk around; let them know who you are. Don't wear a suit; dress casually so they see you as approachable. They already think you make a lot of money as it is. Just meet the people and find out what's going on. Ask what they want to change. In fact, this is a great question to ask tenants *before* you buy a property. In this way, you can find out more than what the management company will tell you.

Making Maintenance Schedules

Be diligent with the management company about setting up a schedule of activities you want it to manage. First and foremost, uniformly set up all your tenants' rents to be due the first of the month. Check management records and processes like clockwork at least twice a month. Be sure to contact your management company reps around the third of the month to see what rents have been collected and what late notices have gone out.

Look at the maintenance record books too. Then drive around the property with the management company rep. Together, make a list of the things that need to be done and then set up a timetable for each task (e.g., mow the lawn every Monday morning; trim the bushes every Tuesday, etc.). It might sound tedious, but these details help you stay on top of managing your property and managing the company itself. They also help you see exactly what's going on and keep close tabs on it.

Clean Up on Mondays

I recommend requiring the grounds maintenance to be completed on Mondays, because trash typically piles up over the weekend. By having the grounds cleaned on Mondays, it will look good during the times prospective tenants usually visit apartments early in the week. In the same vein, don't clean the grounds on Fridays. Why not? Because people usually don't look at apartments on Thursdays and Fridays; they come Mondays and Tuesdays after seeing your ad in the Sunday paper. Often they want to move in immediately, on a Friday or Saturday, so they can settle in and feel ready to get back to their job on Monday. That's the typical cycle.

Once you set a maintenance schedule for the management company to follow, there will then be no reasons for miscommunication. Also, note how to handle the trash. I suggest making sure it's kept in the back of the building. For some reason, superintendents like to keep the trash up front, believing that tenants are more likely to dump their trash as they leave the building. But consider the curb appeal. If a prospective tenant comes in and sees dirty garbage cans in the front, it doesn't leave a good impression. You're better off placing the cans in the back or on the side of the building.

Keep clutter around the building to a minimum. When your property starts to show clutter, it loses its curb appeal and potentially loses new tenants for you.

Lower Maintenance Costs

Get your expenses down per unit. Look at per-unit costs and find ways to get them down. In your building, try to bring them down $18 a unit. If you do that, you'll increase your building's market value by 10 percent. So on a $200,000 building, if you can drop your per-unit cost by $18, you've increased the market value $20,000 *per year*! On larger buildings, that percentage comes out to a lot—even into the millions.

Here's a basic list of minor maintenance issues that will decrease costs:

- Change showerheads to maintain a low-flow, efficient stream of water.
- Get flush valves for the toilets to reduce water use. Water is one of your biggest expenditures.
- For anywhere water comes out, purchase gaskets that adjust the pressure into a spray instead of a full flow. Tenants get the same effect with half the water, which equals half the water use plus reducing the cost of heating water substantially.
- Check light bulbs. You don't need 100-watt bulbs everywhere. Replace them with 60-watt bulbs.
- Seal windows and doors to save on heating and cooling.

These things sound minor, but they add up, especially in big buildings. Understand that even though the savings of these repairs might not show up in small buildings, you're training yourself to manage the large properties you'll soon own. So don't develop bad habits managing the smaller buildings. It's easy to get away with neglecting the details on smaller buildings.

Dealing with Major and Minor Maintenance Issues

You can sometimes get free roofs, free boilers, and low-cost windows for middle- to low-income buildings through the federal government programs. (Some states call this program by a different name, so check with http://www.HUD.org or http://www.LargeRealEstate.com.) The program provides these improvements because they're the biggest expenses—and the most necessary. Their importance is clear: If boilers and hot water heaters in the building don't work, tenants won't have heat or hot water.

Even if you're getting new windows in a couple of months, seal everything up as tightly as possible. Check for good seals around windows and doors, especially in older buildings. For just a little bit of money, you can caulk the windows and seal the doors with a felt liner to keep the building cooler in the summer and warmer in the winter. Don't ever wait to repair or replace the seals. Doing it immediately will save you a lot of money in the long run.

Managing Construction

Rehabbing an apartment building is completely different from rehabbing a house. Besides the difference in scope, there is a difference in details that only experience can teach you. For example, for a house you often want carpeting whereas for an apartment building it's cheaper in the long run to have hardwood floors. And although anything above the first floor needs carpeting for preventing noise, the law stipulates that tenants must provide it, not the landlord.

I recommend hiring a construction manager when doing construction or rehab on a building to educate you about these details and keep an eye on all the contractors who will be coming and going. Your manager can oversee the timetable and communicate with the contractors on the progress of the job, especially if it's running behind. He can also save you money by buying all the materials directly instead of getting them through contractors, who routinely charge markup fees.

G*iving* B*onus* F*ees*

Consider implementing a bonus system when you're working with contractors. For example, have them set up their normal date of completion, but don't tell them there's a bonus system involved. Say the project finish date is October 18. In September, sit down with them and say, "Okay, are you pretty comfortable with that October 18 completion date? Do you need any more time?" Whatever you agree to, write down that revised date and put it in the contract. At that time, tell them there's a bonus if they finish early and a penalty if they finish late.

The amount of the bonus you give is up to you. You can increase it week by week; that is, the earlier they get done, the greater the bonus they get. One way to come up with that number is based on the time value of money. For example, the construction team is working on a 50-unit apartment building, and the workers finish three weeks ahead of schedule. That translates into three more weeks of collecting rent on those units. Calculate the extra rent totals and give them a portion of that unplanned income.

It's important that you and your manager pay attention to when the materials are coming in. The job could be progressing right on time, then stop short because the materials aren't there.

For 10- to 25-unit buildings, make sure someone takes responsibility for having the needed materials on hand at least one week ahead of using them. When dealing with 50-unit and larger buildings, have materials delivered two to three weeks beforehand.

When you put together a timetable with your contractors and construction manager, they should be able to tell you when each phase will be completed. Make sure they tell you exactly what gets completed each week. Always be involved with timetables from the beginning. Don't wait until one week before the deadline to become concerned about making that deadline because, at that point, it's already too late.

Checking on the Management Company

When you first own a building, I recommend meeting with your management company representatives on the first and third Monday of every month. Start early in the morning so you have all day to maximize your time. Go through all the records. Walk around the building and see what kind of shape it's in. Take copies of the books with you and check to make sure recorded costs are legitimate. For example, if the books indicate the maintenance crew painted the hallway, check to see if it's been freshly painted. If the company's rep told you workers are consistently cleaning the hallways, check that too. Some management companies make money by saying they're doing things they aren't; they charge you $300 to paint the walls, but all they asked the workers to do was wipe them down.

After three to six months of that regular routine, break it up. Let your consistency level drop off. So instead of going in on Monday, go in on a Friday. Then get to a point where you say, for instance, "I can't make it in next week. I'll give you a call and let you know when I'm coming." Your goal is to have them relax a bit. They'll be glad that intense period is over with, writing it off as new-owner behavior. Let it fall off for three or four months, but don't let it go too long because their slacking off can cost you a lot of money.

Then do a surprise inspection. Don't tell them you're coming. And don't go to the management company first. Go directly to the building and inspect it. If everything is in great shape, give the reps a call and let them know you're grateful for their diligence. If things are in bad shape, give them a call and let them know they need to shape up. Call them from the property and then go to the management company's office to check the records.

I like to do surprise inspections later in the week, so there are no excuses. If you go on a Monday, for example, and see trash in the front, the management company reps can wave it off, saying it was scheduled to be handled later that day.

If you find various things wrong with the building, make a list before you call the management company. Then when you call, say, "I'm over at the building. There are some issues here. The front door is ajar; there is garbage all over the front," and so on. Read through your entire list. Then tell them, "Send someone over here immediately. I'm waiting at the building." If you go to the office first and ask them to send someone over to deal with the items on the list, it will take a day or two to get action. You're a client of theirs and you're going to wait. Give them a copy of the list. Then go to the management company and look at the books.

You should only have to take this drastic action once. Then you can go every four months—just keep them guessing about what day you'll come again.

DEVELOP A TRACK RECORD

Remember, with the small buildings you own, you're developing a track record and good habits to transfer to large buildings. Although it would save money to have a live-in manager manage the small buildings rather than hiring a management company, the downside is that you're not building a relationship with a company. Not knowing a company you can trust could hurt you down the road, particularly when you go for financing on bigger deals.

A management company can make a big difference in what kinds of properties you can purchase when you start getting that $2 million net worth. Lenders ask, "Who is managing the property?" If you answer, "I've got this guy, Jim, who's been managing these 20 units. So I'm going to have him manage the 100 units," that doesn't inspire as much confidence as saying, "I use XYZ Management Company, which has managed several large apartment buildings in this area for 12 years."

I suggest always dealing with a professional management company as an integral part of your team.

12

PUTTING IT ALL TOGETHER

When I played football at Temple University, we played spring ball to get ready for our regular season. During the spring practice season, each team member individually practiced the basics—running, tackling, and catching the ball. Then, at practice season's end, we'd put together all those skills to form plays. It was critical for each player to have a successful preseason in order to do well in the conference games.

Any good coach understands the basics. When a team has a problem, the coach automatically goes back to the basics, even in the middle of the regular season. In fact, good coaches go back to running only 4 or 5 plays instead of their usual 120. They want to put the basics solidly back in place before moving on.

I believe in following a formula that keeps practicing basics, just as I did years ago on Temple's football team. So far, you've studied them in previous chapters. Now it's time to put them all together. If you need a refresher for any one aspect, refer to the following list and see what needs reviewing. After that, no excuses. Just get moving.

Chapter 1: Why Invest in Apartment Buildings

- This book is about residential commercial property, defined by lenders as five units or more. Commercial properties offer investors massive leverage, the type that builds long-term passive wealth. The more units you own, the more potential wealth you'll have; it's that simple.

- Banks don't want to lend a little bit of money; they prefer lending a lot of money. Gaining wealth in real estate is about buying large properties. This is ideal, because as much as we want to own these large properties, lenders want us to buy them.

- Discussion in this book focuses on 10 to 25 units and refers to properties that are easily obtainable to build momentum. The momentum gets going for investors and lenders as the money accumulates on bigger and bigger deals.

- With commercial property, a lender examines the financial aspects of the property first and scrutinizes the borrower second. It's ideal when lenders are more interested in a property than they are in the investor(s). Be sure to view commercial real estate investing as a business because that's the way the "money" views it.

- Lenders are proficient at determining not only whether the building can pay for both its operating expenses and its debt service (the commercial term for mortgage), but also whether the owner can make money from the purchase. Commercial real estate is analyzed by the amount of cash, the monetary income that the property generates. To crunch those numbers, lenders use a cash flow analysis formula.

- Creditworthiness means having a track record that indicates loans are repaid and bills paid. When lenders examine investors, they're concerned with their track records. If you don't have a track record, find someone who does. Don't regard the lack of a track record as a stumbling block but rather as a solution. In real estate investing, there's a creative solution to everything.

- Invest in middle- to low-income (or affordable) housing because it generates cash flow. It's preferable because of its low purchase price compared with the relatively high amount of rent it generates.

Chapter 2: Setting the Location Strategy

- How do you map out your area to find your ideal property? No successful team wins a championship without a game plan. Locate your field of play and focus on it to increase your success ratio.
- Search for Economic Development Zones; stay away from economically *challenged* zones. Concentrate on areas that want and need help from investors, which translates directly into opportunities for you.
- Find communities that have the highest need for Section 8 housing. Providing such housing is a great way to help the community and build wealth. In certain areas, you can even command market rates for Section 8 tenants.
- Locate safe, clean neighborhoods near malls that have an active anchor store and successful filler stores. Locating near anchors and fillers can come in handy when a tenant needs a new job or a second income to pay the rent in addition to providing convenient shopping for tenants. But more important, anchors indicate where the smart money is being invested in communities. You can piggyback on the research of others to boost your real estate investing portfolio.

Chapter 3: Locating the Right Property

- Start with the old standby: call from newspaper ads placed by commercial real estate brokers. From these ads, you can at least tell what types of properties are available and what the overall market looks like. You probably won't find the gems you want in the newspaper, but seeking leads from newspaper ads is an efficient way to research the market and even locate team members to partner with.
- Contact real estate brokers, management companies, and other investors to help you locate good properties. Remember, although contacting real estate brokers can be effective, they're not the only game in town. To put together the ideal portfolio, I suggest establishing a network of real estate professionals.

Chapter 4: Analyzing the Deal

- Get started by reviewing the property setup sheet, which is the first information that comes from a potential team member and your first look at a potential deal. Learn to read between the lines by noting information you receive on this particular property and then compare it to the original property setup. Pros gain considerable insight from a little information.
- Because it's all based on the numbers, get to know what a property is worth from the cash flow analysis. Here are the main ingredients to study and dream about in your sleep.
  - Vacancy allowance
  - Collections allowance
  - Effective gross income (EGI)
  - Management fee
  - Operating expenses
  - Net operating income (NOI)

- Debt service
- Cash flow
- Have the tools of a pro at your fingertips. Be sure to purchase a good real estate calculator and carry it with you at all times; you never know when you'll find a deal. If you want the next level of expertise, you can get the REAPAC™ program that does the calculation work for you. (You can order it at http://www.LargeRealEstate.com.) It has a proprietary 13-step formula integrated into it. In addition, get a fax machine. Without it, how can sellers immediately say yes to your offers?
- You need to deal with all aspects of the properties you buy, including such potential problems as asbestos and lead paint. Know where they may show up, but have a professional check them out; it's worth the cost to be sure.

Chapter 5: Gathering More Details

- High rises. Town houses. Apartment buildings. Every piece of real estate has its advantages and disadvantages. Knowing the strengths and weaknesses of investing in each can make you successful. Carve out your niche early in your investing career.
- To determine market rents and income, check out government Web sites that can give you the median income for areas of interest. Make sure you know what existing rents are exactly, or you won't be able to figure out your cash flow analysis.
- Expenses can be the trickiest part of your analysis. Use your 40 percent rule or contact a key team member and find out accurate numbers to determine profitability.
- Net operating income *is* the property. Everything you do in real estate revolves around this number, so make sure to do your homework and check your numbers twice.

Chapter 6: Using Creative Financing

- Build a strong financial team with aggressive mortgage brokers.
- Working with private money allows you to be more flexible. If those lenders are happy with the deals you bring them, they'll insist on giving you more money.
- Creative financing strategies come from creative thinkers. If you know in your heart that you can get the deal done, then you'll find a way. Start with the right "can do" mind-set.

Chapter 7: Structuring the Offer and Negotiating

- Find the best interest rates available. Would you rather *pay* compounding interest or *receive* compounding interest? If your credit isn't stellar, take on a partner who has a sound credit record.
- Writing solid purchase contracts separates the boys and girls from the men and women. The first investor to get a contract out usually wins the race.
- Writing your addenda to the purchase contract is the cheapest insurance you'll ever buy. If you're uneasy about any situation concerning the property or the seller, put together an addendum to handle it. It's your secret weapon.
- Writing offers is your bread and butter. If you don't make an offer, you can't buy a property. It's that simple. So make lots of offers.

Chapter 8: Forming Partnerships

- Partnerships are composed of three different variables. From these, you can make an unlimited number of partnership agreements.

- I suggest dealing with only one partner, even if that partner is a group of people.
- Forming limited partnerships can be tricky. Follow the guidelines outlined in this book.
- Paying investors is a form of exchange. Figure out what amount of payment is available from the building proceeds and pay all partners according to the arrangement you set up when forming the partnership.

Chapter 9: Working with a Team

- Those who play on the best team always win. Build a strong investment team so your investments can bring you the wealth you desire.
- Start with one team member, analyze that person's performance, and make necessary adjustments. From there, add team members as necessary.
- Success means change. As you become more successful, so does everyone on your team. You might want to change team members as your business grows and flourishes. And never exchange your heart for a bank account in the name of success.

Chapter 10. Closing on the Property

- One of your closing strategies might be to never go to the closing. Reread this chapter to review the reason.
- Never skip building inspections. Before the property becomes yours, find out what the previous owners have been doing with it over the span of years.
- Working with management companies can be the smartest move you'll ever make. Work with those that show brains and experience.

- The art of negotiation can be learned from great books, including those written by Herb Cohen. Read them!

Chapter 11. Managing the Building

- Construction bills come out of your pocket. Be meticulous about who you hire, manage the work closely, and ask lots of questions.
- To manage the management company, watch what its representatives do and observe how their style works for everyone involved. Refer back to this chapter often, especially if anything isn't going right with the way the building is being run.
- Make detailed schedules to handle maintenance issues in a businesslike way. Don't leave building management and maintenance to chance.
- Learn how to deal with Section 8 tenants, and you've got a profitable niche. You're helping people who get assistance from the government, and help is a good thing.

Just like any great athlete you need to practice the basics, so read through this book as many times as possible and utilize the resources I put together for you, such as http://www.LargeReal Estate.com and http://www.GregWarr.com. As my grandfather told me, "You have to ask in order to get a YES!"

Read on to the final chapter. You'll learn how real estate can support a charity for life!

13

GIVING BACK

A friend and I were discussing the definition of wealth. To him, wealth means *having such an abundance of money that money would never be an issue.* For me, it's *never having to want for anything.* That means having all the information and tools necessary to build whatever I want, whenever I want it. I think that's even more important than simply having money in the bank.

Some people have become wealthy by being in the right place at the right time. There's nothing wrong with operating on luck, but do you think those people who rely on it actually feel secure? There's a chance they live in fear because if they run out of money, they might never experience that so-called luck again. Therefore, I look at wealth this way: if I can produce a desired result almost at will, then I'm a wealthy person.

Giving you that phenomenal gift—the ability to build what I want through real estate—was exactly my intention in writing this book. Providing others with the tools to make their own money can become your reason too—besides creating wealth for yourself. You'll see that making money is simple, although it might not be easy. Why is that true? Because you actually have to do something—take that first fearful step. But if you use this book to develop a detailed game plan designed to create wealth, then it all comes down to applying your plan step-by-step.

Please understand I have no problem with my friend's definition of making an abundance of money. But at the end of the day, *what really matters is what you do with that money.*

GAINING CONTROL

Have you ever noticed that the help you give to others is similar to assistance you've received first—such as getting a call from a friend when you needed it most? People not only need to help themselves; they also need to give help to others—and enjoy hearing expressions of gratitude for doing so.

Help becomes available when someone has the ability to control a specific situation. *Control* can be an ugly word when people use it in an ugly way. But there's something beautiful about gaining control over your life and using it to move forward. Applying control this way communicates to others that you know how to get what you want and can help others achieve what they need. When you say this to the right sources, they'll support whatever you're trying to do.

The converse is true, too; if you don't control what you have, things don't get better; they only get worse. Let's take a piece of real estate as an example. If you purchased a run-down building, rehabbed it, and filled it with satisfied tenants, then never touched it again for 20 years, you'd have a slum on your hands. So even starting out with the best intentions but not following through changes nothing. Besides, don't you want to create wealth by changing things for the better?

How I'm Helping to Change

In the five years I've been involved in real estate, I've been afforded many opportunities and have taken advantage of several—not only making profitable real estate deals but writing this book. I've traveled around the country teaching others what I've learned about real estate. I'm very appreciative of people who want to spend their time listening to what I have to say about real estate. It's quite an honor for me.

In the beginning, however, I wasn't up to the challenge. A number of times in the early years, people asked me to speak about what I'd learned. At first, I'm embarrassed to say, I said no. At that time, I probably didn't look at it from the viewpoint of giving. You see, I cringe even now when I see a TV commercial showing a struggling, fatigued business traveler. Maybe I was a pack mule in a past life, but I hate the idea of trudging through airports and lugging things around with me. Despite that image, I've now learned to enjoy traveling, and I always look forward to my next trip.

When I decided to start teaching what I'd learned, of course I wanted to accomplish several things at one time. First, because I'd never traveled much in my youth, I wanted to expand my personal horizons and see the country. Next, I wanted to expand my business horizons and learn what people in other parts of the country were doing in real estate. (At that point, I was only buying real estate in New York, specifically the five burroughs.) I soon was amazed at the opportunities available—not only learning how much money is available but also how it's spent developing real estate opportunities.

Wealth and Poverty Side by Side

Along with finding exciting opportunities in my travels, I also discovered how bad many situations are. It's a strange dichotomy—observing extreme wealth coexisting with dire poverty and destruction, many times right next door to each other. From my observation, it seems that illiteracy is a strong factor in creating and perpetuating these bad situations.

This might sound simplistic, but I strongly believe these statements to be true: If someone can't read, his or her life will be extremely difficult, if not impossible. People who are illiterate in this country must work ten times harder to compensate for their inability to read. I believe that a lot of illiterate people have the drive and energy to succeed, but lacking the ability to read holds them back. I also think that a large (if not all-encompassing) problem in the prison system stems from illiteracy or people having an extremely hard time reading and understanding the English language. Some might think it's a stretch to correlate illiteracy with such crimes as robbery and murder, but I honestly believe a direct relationship exists.

Lowering Levels of Education

What first caught my attention about the education problem in this country was the generational discrepancy in vocabulary and basic knowledge. When I talk to people from a generation older than mine (including my business partner who's in his 60s), the difference in the quality of education each of us received is apparent—mine much lower than his. (I hate to admit this because I consider myself an intelligent individual.) But I think the trend continues into younger generations. Most people graduating from high school today don't have the level of education I had.

I see this growing ignorance displayed on late-night TV shows when hosts go to the streets and interview passersby who don't even know the name of the president of the United States. Some might call that entertainment, but is it really funny not knowing who runs your country, or how to do basic math to balance a checkbook, or how to apply writing skills to daily living? These are serious issues for a lot of people today. Without getting on a soapbox, I want to communicate how strongly I feel about this situation throughout this chapter.

EDUCATION AND REAL ESTATE

What does a lower level of education have to do with real estate? I believe people need a better education, and I want to help them by using the real estate vehicles I have at my fingertips.

Not long ago, I saw my opportunity. I made an appointment to meet with the city and district planners in a major American city to discuss Section 8 housing. When I sat down with these officials, I started dazzling them with my real estate knowledge and portfolio. But after I had spent 40 minutes doing my song and dance, I realized they couldn't have cared less about my real estate prowess. I was wrong to try to impress them with my résumé. Clearly, the question I needed to ask them was, "What can I do to help *you?*" And you know, once I asked the question, I found out exactly what they needed in the span of five seconds.

They told me that although putting in Section 8 housing would help the city, their immediate concern was the prison system—their primary focus at that point. My asking "How can I help?" opened the floodgates for them. They brought up the subject of transitional housing, which I knew little about. They said, "When people come out of prison, they go into a transitional house for about six months. In those six months, they are supposed to make a transition back into society, open bank accounts, and get jobs while integrating into the community.

"The problem is the people still live there three years after getting out of prison—two and a half years too long. Now, they haven't done anything wrong; they just haven't progressed in creating a new life for themselves as quickly as planned. With that problem arise bigger ones—where do newly released prisoners go? Should the system keep them in prison longer? How is it decided which ones go into transitional housing and which ones get released into the community immediately?" They asked these questions and more as they laid out the problems.

Hearing this, my ethical and humanitarian principles kicked in. Having become aware of this, I knew I had to do something about it. So again I asked, "How can I help?" They said, "You could start building more transitional housing in this city."

Recidivism Rates

Soon after, I learned about a nonprofit organization that's had great success working with people coming out of the prison system. In this city, the recidivism rate (the percentage of people who go back to prison because they commit a new crime) was above 85 percent. However, the recidivism rate for prisoners that this nonprofit organization worked with actually reversed the city's numbers. For those who went through its programs, the success rate was 85 percent, with the recidivism rate only 15 percent.

How was this organization able to turn the statistics around completely? By realizing that most prisoners are on drugs and the typical way to deal with people on drugs—to give them a new drug—doesn't work. Therefore, this organization bases its rehab program on using no drugs at all.

In addition to providing a nondrug, drug rehab program, people in this nonprofit group teach former prisoners how to read. Basically, the ability to read and write well is the ability to communicate effectively. You might have heard people say, "That guy refuses to communicate." But isn't "refusal" actually a form of communicating? Isn't it letting people know you don't want to talk to them? In my book, *everything* people do relates to communication—from the way they walk to the way they talk.

Have you ever been so frustrated and angry that all you wanted was to feel listened to by others? You didn't necessarily want to get an answer to your problem; you just wanted to be heard—a process that can be highly therapeutic. However, if people can't communicate their problems well, those frustrations build up. Although you might communicate by sitting down and having a logical and meaningful conversation, a criminal might go into a liquor store, hit someone on the head with a bat, and take money as a form of communication.

Do you see how helping others expand their ability to express themselves verbally and through reading and writing provides tools for better communication and less frustration?

ALIGNING WITH A NONPROFIT

As you read in earlier chapters, I believe in building teams and employing people's strengths. In this transitional housing situation, I saw an opportunity to do just that—in partnership with the nonprofit group mentioned earlier. I would provide the real estate and structure the program, and the people in the nonprofit would implement its nondrug, drug rehab, and literacy programs. You see, I'm not looking to reinvent the wheel; I just want to make it spin faster.

As a result, I devised a three-phase approach. But before I could do that, I had to determine whom I intended to help. Specifically, I decided to deal with prisoners who were nonviolent, nonsexual offenders. That includes people who have done just plain stupid things—such as buying lots of drugs for themselves and friends and then making good money selling the rest. Also, I

decided to target prisoners who have spouses and children because I want to help entire families change the environments in
which they live. In addition, I feel strongly about continuing to
provide literacy programs to the children.

THREE-PHASE PROCESS

Here's how the three-phase program is designed to work:

First phase. In the first phase, prisoners come out of jail and
move into the transitional housing I've built. They're told about
the program that's run by my nonprofit partner and agree to
participate in it as a condition of living in this housing development. In this first phase, they go through the complete nondrug,
drug rehab program because it's essential for them to get the tox-
ins out of their system to feel more energized and think more
clearly. It's also critical that they realize going through the program will take hard work on their part.

Once they've cleared that hurdle, they learn how to learn. Yes,
that's correct—during their life, most of them haven't been taught
how to learn new things. In fact, I'd venture to say few people have
gone through courses like this. *Most people go through elementary
school, high school, and college without ever having been taught how to
learn independently.*

In this program, participants learn such basic skills as keeping
themselves and their clothes clean, caring for their immediate environment, and caring for the people around them—basically, the
skills they need to get along in society. It takes each participant as
long as required to complete the program, because each person
responds differently. But the statistics show that most participants
complete it in less than six months. Not only have they learned to
learn, they usually come away feeling happier.

Second phase. The people I intend to help are those who have families. What good is it to rehabilitate people and then put them back into their old environment? When they go back into a familiar environment that sets up a powerful challenge at a time when they're most likely to return to their old ways. Also, statistics show that if one spouse is doing drugs, there's a 94 or greater percent chance that the other spouse does drugs too. So in the second phase, the spouses also go through a nondrug, drug rehab program. They learn how to take care of themselves and their environment, and they also participate in literacy programs.

How many strikes do you think children of these newly released prisoners have against them? You can see how living in a situation with parents who use drugs can become a downward spiral for the kids in the family. So this second phase includes having their kids go through the children's learning and literacy programs. More than that, through this partnership we're helping these children by giving them "transformed" parents who aren't in prison, who aren't on drugs, and who are productive members of society.

Once the family has learned to work well together and integrate into their community, it's time for them to move on to the third phase.

Make Education the Norm

Every so often, a kid who comes from a broken home gets an education and earns scholarships, sometimes even to Ivy League universities. I think it's time to make that experience the norm in this country.

Third phase. Sometimes the government uses a catchword: homeownership. That's what the third phase is all about. Because the participants already went through drug rehab in the first phase and are well into literacy programs after the second phase, they're able to get jobs and start bringing home income at the same time spouses go through the program in the third phase. A lot of these people not only need jobs but also to learn employable skills. When they do, steady employment leads to homeownership, which often moves them out of transitional housing in less than the year that was planned.

In this third phase, homeownership satisfies a number of different factors. First, it stops people from going back into their old environment, and it helps them relocate. That doesn't mean they shouldn't visit their old neighborhoods to share what they've learned, but it simply doesn't work for them to return and resume their former lifestyle there.

With increasing numbers of people going through this program, an increasing number of housing units consequently need to be built. Many learn skills related to construction—not only because building something with their own hands helps build morale, but the emotional rewards for building one's own home can be huge. It can even change a person's life completely. (Currently, I'm researching and testing new building materials to speed up this building process. Any input would be greatly appreciated. Yes, I'm asking for your help.)

I could even say there's a fourth phase to this. But the participants today will have to define what that fourth phase will look like.

MAKING A DIFFERENCE

After I formulated this strategy to serve families of newly released prisoners, I presented it to the city's district planner, who said, "If you implement these programs and get half the results statistically that you're talking about, I can 'donate' city-owned land and buildings for a low price. That allows you to do this on as large a scale as you want."

At this time, we're starting out small to build a track record and gather more statistics. Yet because the nonprofit that's implementing the nondrug drug rehab and literacy programs has gathered years of statistics, I'm certain our statistics will be similar going forward. We run tests, gather more data, and add statistics to the nonprofit's proven track record.

I share this "giving back" idea to show you what can be done with the real estate information I've given you throughout this book. Making money is fine, but *making a difference* is really what gets people out of bed each morning.

Where do *you* want to take this information? How will *you* give to others and make a difference in the world?

You decide; you're in control of creating your own wealth—however you define it.

To learn more about this process, go to http://www.Large RealEstate.com and click on *charities*.

Commercial Speak

A

abatement Often and commonly referred to as free rent or early occupancy and may occur outside or in addition to the primary term of the lease.

above building standard Upgraded finishes and specialized designs necessary to accommodate a tenant's requirements.

absorption The rate, expressed as a percentage, at which available space in the marketplace is leased during a predetermined period of time. Also referred to as *market absorption*.

absorption rate The net change in space available for lease between two dates, typically expressed as a percentage of the total square footage.

ad valorem According to value. This is a tax imposed on the value of property (references a general property tax), which is typically based on the local government's valuation of the property.

add-on factor Often referred to as the *loss factor* or *rentable/usable (R/U) factor*, it represents the tenant's pro-rata share of the building common areas, such as lobbies, public corridors, and restrooms. It is usually expressed as a percentage that can then be applied to the usable square footage to determine the rentable square footage on which the tenant will pay rent.

allowance over building shell Most often used in a yet-to-be constructed property, the tenant has a blank canvas on which to customize the interior finishes to its specifications. This arrangement caps the landlord's expenditure at a fixed dollar amount over the negotiated price of the base building shell.

This arrangement is most successful when both parties agree on a detailed definition of what construction is included and at what price.

anchor tenant The major or prime tenant in a shopping center, building, etc.

annual percentage rate (APR) The actual cost of borrowing money, expressed in the form of an annual interest rate. It may be higher than the note rate, because it represents full disclosure of the interest rate, loan origination fees, loan discount points, and other credit costs paid to the lender.

appraisal An estimate of opinion and value based on a factual analysis of a property by a qualified professional.

appreciation The increased value of an asset.

"as-is" condition The acceptance by the tenant of the existing condition of the premises at the time the lease is consummated. This would include any physical defects.

assessment A fee imposed on property, usually to pay for public improvements such as water, sewers, streets, improvement districts, etc.

assignment A transfer by lessee of lessee's entire estate in the property. Distinguishable from a sublease, where the sublessee acquires something less than the lessee's entire interest.

attorn To turn over or transfer to another money or goods. To agree to recognize a new owner of a property and to pay him or her rent. In a lease, when the tenant agrees to *attorn* to the purchaser, the landlord is given the power to subordinate tenant's interest to any first mortgage or deed of trust lien subsequently placed on the leased premises.

B

balloon payment A large principal payment that typically becomes due at the conclusion of the loan term. Generally, it reflects a loan amortized over a longer period than that of the term of the loan itself (i.e., payments based on a 25-year amortization with the principal balance due at the end of 5 years). See also *bullet loan*.

bankrupt The condition or state of a person (individual, partnership, corporation, etc.) who is unable to repay his or her debts as they are, or become, due.

bankruptcy Proceedings under federal statutes to relieve a debtor who is unable or unwilling to pay its debts. After addressing certain priorities and exemptions, the bankrupt's property and other assets are distributed by the court to creditors as full satisfaction for the debt. See also *Chapter 11*.

base rent A set amount used as a minimum rent in a lease with provisions for increasing the rent over the term of the lease. See also *escalation clause, operating expense escalation,* and *percentage lease*.

base year Actual taxes and operating expenses for a specified base year, most often the year in which the lease commences. Once the base year expenses are known, the lease essentially becomes a dollar stop lease.

below-grade Any structure or a portion of a structure located underground or below the surface grade of the surrounding land.

building classifications Building classifications in most markets refer to Class A, B, C, and sometimes D properties. While the rating assigned to a particular building is very subjective, Class A properties are typically newer buildings with superior construction and finish in excellent locations with easy access and are attractive to credit tenants, and offer a multitude of amenities, such as on-site management or covered parking. These buildings, of course, command the highest rental rates in their submarket. As the class of the building decreases (i.e., Class B, C, or D), one component or another, such as age, location, or construction of the building, becomes less desirable. Note that a Class A building in one submarket might rank lower if it were located in a distinctly different submarket just a few miles away containing a higher-end product.

building code The various laws set forth by the ruling municipality as to the end use of a certain piece of property and that dictate the criteria for design, materials, and type of improvements allowed.

building or "core" factor Represents the percentage of net rentable square feet devoted to the building's common areas (lobbies, restrooms, corridors, etc.). This factor can be computed for an entire building or a single floor of a building. Also known as loss factor or rentable/usable (R/U) factor, it is calculated by dividing the rentable square footage by the usable square footage. See also *rentable/usable ratio.*

building standard A list of construction materials and finishes that represents what the tenant improvement (finish) allowance/ workletter is designed to cover, while also serving to establish the landlord's minimum quality standards with respect to tenant finish improvements within the building. Examples of standard building items are type and style of doors, lineal feet of partitions, quantity of lights, quality of floor covering, etc.

building standard plus allowance The landlord lists, in detail, the building standard materials and costs necessary to make the premises suitable for occupancy. A negotiated allowance is then provided for the tenant to customize or upgrade materials. See also *workletter.*

build-out The space improvements put in place per the tenant's specifications. Takes into consideration the amount of tenant finish allowance provided for in the lease agreement. See also *tenant improvement allowance.*

build-to-suit An approach taken to lease space by a property owner where a new building is designed and constructed per the tenant's specifications.

bullet loan Any short-term, generally five to seven years, financing option that requires a balloon payment at the end of the term and anticipates that the loan will be refinanced in order to meet the balloon payment obligation. Essentially, should the refinancing not be available, often due to the property not performing as anticipated, the borrower is "shot," and the property is subject to foreclosure. An example of this would be a developer that borrows to cover the costs of construction and carry-costs for a new building with the expectation that it would be replaced by long-term (or "permanent") financing provided by an institutional investor once most of the risk involved in construction and lease-up had been overcome, resulting in an income-producing property.

C

capital expenses This type of expense is most often defined by reference to generally accepted accounting principles (GAAP), but GAAP does not provide definitive guidance on all possible expenditures. Accountants will often disagree on whether or not to include certain items.

capitalization A method of determining value of real property by considering net operating income divided by a predetermined annual rate of return. See also *capitalization rate.*

capitalization rate The rate that is considered a reasonable return on investment (on the basis of both the investor's alternative investment possibilities and the risk of the investment). Used to determine and value real property through the capitalization process. Also called *free and clear return.* See also *capitalization.*

carrying charges Costs incidental to property ownership, other than interest (i.e., taxes, insurance costs, and maintenance expenses), that must be absorbed by the landlord during the initial lease-up of a building and thereafter during periods of vacancy.

certificate of occupancy A document presented by a local government agency or building department certifying that a building and/or the leased premises (tenant's space) has been satisfactorily inspected and is/are in a condition suitable for occupancy.

Chapter 7 That portion of the federal bankruptcy code that deals with business liquidations.

Chapter 11 That portion of the federal bankruptcy code that deals with business reorganizations.

clear-span facility A building, most often a warehouse or parking garage, with vertical columns on the outside edges of the structure and a clear span between columns.

circulation factor Interior space required for internal office circulation not accounted for in the net square footage. Based on our experience, we use a circulation factor of 1.35 times the net square footage for office and fixed drywall areas and a circulation factor of 1.45 times the net square footage for open area workstations. See also *net square footage* and *usable square footage.*

common area There are two components of the term *common area.* If referred to in association with the rentable/usable or load factor calculation, the common areas are those areas within a building that are available for common use by all tenants or groups of tenants and their invitees (i.e., lobbies, corridors, restrooms, etc.). On the other hand, the cost of maintaining parking facilities, malls, sidewalks, landscaped areas, public toilets, truck and service facilities, and the like are included in the term *common area* when calculating the tenant's pro-rata share of building operating expenses.

common area maintenance (CAM) This is the amount of additional rent charged to the tenant, in addition to the base rent, to maintain the common areas of the property shared by the tenants and from which all tenants benefit. Examples include snow removal, outdoor lighting, parking lot sweeping, insurance, property taxes, etc. Most often, this does not include any capital improvements (see *capital expenses*) that are made to the property.

comparables Lease rates and terms of properties similar in size, construction quality, age, use, and typically located within the same submarket and used as comparison properties to determine the fair market lease rate for another property with similar characteristics.

concessions Cash or cash equivalents expended by the landlord in the form of rental abatement, additional tenant finish allowance, moving expenses, cabling expenses, or other monies expended to influence or persuade the tenant to sign a lease.

condemnation The process of taking private property, without the consent of the owner, by a governmental agency for public use through the power of eminent domain. See also *eminent domain.*

construction management The actual construction process is overseen by a qualified construction manager who ensures that the various stages of the construction process are completed in a timely and seamless fashion, from getting the construction permit to completion of the construction to the final walkthrough of the completed leased premises with the tenant.

consumer price index (CPI) Measures inflation in relation to the change in the price of a fixed market basket of goods and services purchased by a specified population during a "base" period of time. It is not a true "cost of living" factor and bears little direct relation to actual costs of building operation or the value of real estate. The CPI is commonly used to increase the base rental periodically as a means of protecting the landlord's rental stream against inflation or to provide a cushion for operating expense increases for a landlord unwilling to undertake the recordkeeping necessary for operating expense escalations.

contiguous space (1) Multiple suites/spaces within the same building and on the same floor that can be combined and rented to a single tenant. (2) A block of space located on multiple adjoining floors in a building (i.e., a tenant leases floors 6 through 12 in a building).

contract documents The complete set of design plans and specifications for the construction of a building or of a building's interior improvements. Working drawings specify for the contractor the precise manner in which a project is to be constructed. See also *specifications* and *working drawings.*

conveyance Most commonly refers to the transfer of title to property between parties by deed. The term may also include most of the instruments by which an interest in real estate is created, mortgaged, or assigned.

core factor Represents the percentage of net rentable square feet devoted to the building's common areas (lobbies, restrooms, corridors, etc.). This factor can be computed for an entire building or a single floor of a building. Also known as a loss factor or rentable/usable (R/U) factor, it is calculated by dividing the rentable square footage by the usable square footage.

cost approach A method of appraising real property whereby the replacement cost of a structure is calculated using current costs of construction.

covenant A written agreement inserted into deeds or other legal instruments stipulating performance or nonperformance of certain acts or uses or nonuse of a property and/or land.

covenant of quiet enjoyment The old "quiet enjoyment" paragraph, now more commonly referred to as *warranty of possession,* had nothing to do with noise in and around the leased premises. It provides a warranty by landlord that it has the legal ability to convey the possession of the premises to tenant;

the landlord does not warrant that he or she owns the land. This is the essence of the landlord's agreement and the tenant's obligation to pay rent. This means that if the landlord breaches this warranty, it constitutes an actual or constructive eviction.

cumulative discount rate The interest rate used in finding present values that when applied to the rental rate takes into account all landlord lease concessions and then is expressed as a percentage of base rent.

D

dedicate To appropriate private property to public ownership for a public use.

deed A legal instrument transferring title to real property from the seller to the buyer on the sale of such property.

deed in lieu of foreclosure A deed given by an owner/borrower to a lender to satisfy a mortgage debt and avoid foreclosure. See also *foreclosure.*

deed of trust An instrument used in many states in place of a mortgage by which real property is transferred to a trustee by the borrower (trustor), in favor of the lender (beneficiary), to secure repayment of a debt.

default The general failure to perform a legal or contractual duty or to discharge an obligation when due. Some specific examples are (1) failure to make a payment of rent when due and (2) the breach or failure to perform any of the terms of a lease agreement.

deficiency judgment Imposition of personal liability on a borrower for the unpaid balance of mortgage debt after a foreclosure has failed to yield the full amount of the debt.

demising walls The partition wall that separates one tenant's space from another or from the building's common area, such as a public corridor.

design/build A system in which a single entity is responsible for both the design and construction. The term can apply to an entire facility or to individual components of the construction to be performed by a subcontractor; also referred to as *design/construct.*

depreciation Spreading out the cost of a capital asset over its estimated useful life or a decrease in the usefulness, and therefore value, of real property improvements or other assets caused by deterioration or obsolescence.

distraint The act of seizing (legally or illegally) personal property based on the right and interest that a landlord has in the property of a tenant in default.

dollar stop An agreed dollar amount of taxes and operating expense (expressed for the building as a whole or on a square foot basis) over which the tenant will pay its prorated share of increases. May be applied to specific expenses (e.g., property taxes or insurance).

E

earnest money The monetary advance by a buyer of part of the purchase price to indicate the intention and ability of the buyer to carry out the contract.

easement A right of use over the property of another created by grant, reservation, agreement, prescription, or necessary implication. It is either for the benefit of adjoining land (*appurtenant*), such as the right to cross A to get to B, or for the benefit of a specific individual (*in gross*), such as a public utility easement.

economic feasibility A building or project's feasibility in terms of costs and revenue, with excess revenue establishing the degree of viability.

economic rent The market rental value of a property at a given point in time, even though the actual rent may be different.

effective rent The actual rental rate to be achieved by the landlord after deducting the value of concessions from the base rental rate paid by a tenant, usually expressed as an average rate over the term of the lease.

efficiency factor Represents the percentage of net rentable square feet devoted to the building's common areas (lobbies, restrooms, corridors, etc.). This factor can be computed for an entire building or a single floor of a building. Also known as a core factor or rentable/usable (R/U) factor, it is calculated by dividing the rentable square footage by the usable square footage.

eminent domain A power of the state, municipalities, and private persons or corporations authorized to exercise functions of public character to acquire private property for public use by condemnation, in return for just compensation. See also *condemnation.*

encroachment The intrusion of a structure which extends, without permission, over a property line, easement boundary, or building setback line.

encumbrance Any right to, or interest in, real property held by someone other than the owner, but that will not prevent the transfer of fee title (i.e., a claim, lien, charge, or liability attached to and binding real property).

environmental impact statement Documents that are required by federal and state laws to accompany proposals for major projects and programs that will likely have an impact on the surrounding environment.

equity The fair market value of an asset less any outstanding indebtedness or other encumbrances.

escalation clause A clause in a lease that provides for the rent to be increased to reflect changes in expenses paid by the landlord, such as real estate taxes, operating costs, etc. This may be accomplished by several means, such as fixed periodic increases,

increases tied to the consumer price index, or adjustments based on changes in expenses paid by the landlord in relation to a dollar stop or base year reference.

estoppel certificate A signed statement certifying that certain statements of fact are correct as of the date of the statement and can be relied on by a third party, including a prospective lender or purchaser. In the context of a lease, a statement by a tenant identifying that the lease is in effect and certifying that no rent has been prepaid and that there are no known outstanding defaults by the landlord (except those specified).

escrow agreement A written agreement made between the parties to a contract and an escrow agent. The escrow agreement sets forth the basic obligations of the parties, describes the monies (or other things of value) to be deposited in escrow, and instructs the escrow agent concerning the disposition of the monies deposited.

exclusive agency listing A written agreement between a real estate broker and a property owner in which the owner promises to pay a fee or commission to the broker if specified real property is leased during the listing period. The broker need not be the procuring cause of the lease.

expense stop An agreed dollar amount of taxes and operating expense (expressed for the building as a whole or on a square-foot basis) over which the tenant will pay its prorated share of increases. May be applied to specific expenses (e.g., property taxes or insurance).

F

face rental rate The "asking" rental rate published by the landlord.

fair market value The sale price at which a property would change hands between a willing buyer and willing seller, neither being under any compulsion to buy or sell and both having reasonable knowledge of the relevant facts. Also known as FMV.

finance charge The amount paid for the privilege deferring payment of goods or services purchased, including any charges payable by the purchaser as a condition of the loan.

first generation space Generally refers to new space that is currently available for lease and has never before been occupied by a tenant. See also *second generation space*.

first mortgage The senior mortgage which, by reason of its position, has priority over all junior encumbrances. The holder of the first or senior mortgage has a priority right to payment in the event of default.

first refusal right or right of first refusal (purchase) A lease clause giving a tenant the first opportunity to buy a property at the same price and on the same terms and conditions as those contained in a third party offer that the owner has expressed a willingness to accept.

first refusal right or right of first refusal (adjacent space) A lease clause giving a tenant the first opportunity to lease additional space that might become available in a property at the same price and on the same terms and conditions as those contained in a third party offer that the owner has expressed a willingness to accept. This right is often restricted to specific areas of the building, such as adjacent suites or other suites on the same floor.

fixed costs Costs, such as rent, that do not fluctuate in proportion to the level of sales or production.

flex space A building providing its occupants the flexibility of utilizing the space. Usually provides a configuration allowing a flexible amount of office or showroom space in combination with manufacturing, laboratory, warehouse distribution, etc. Typically also provides the flexibility to relocate overhead doors. Generally constructed with little or no common areas, load-bearing floors, loading dock facilities, and high ceilings.

floor area ratio (FAR) The ratio of the gross square footage of a building to the land on which it is situated. Calculated by dividing the total square footage in the building by the square footage of land area.

force majeure A force that cannot be controlled by the parties to a contract and prevents said parties from complying with the provisions of the contract. This includes acts of God, such as a flood or a hurricane, or acts of man, such as a strike, fire, or war.

foreclosure A procedure by which the mortgagee (lender) either takes title to or forces the sale of the mortgagor's (borrower) property in satisfaction of a debt. See also *deed in lieu of foreclosure.*

full recourse A loan on which an endorser or guarantor is liable in the event of default by the borrower.

full-service rent An all-inclusive rental rate that includes operating expenses and real estate taxes for the first year. The tenant is generally still responsible for any increase in operating expenses over the base year amount. See also *pass throughs.*

future proposed space Space in a proposed commercial development that is not yet under construction or where no construction start date has been set. Future proposed projects include all those projects waiting for a lead tenant, financing, zoning, approvals, or any other event necessary to begin construction. Also may refer to the future phases of a multiphase project not yet built.

G

general contractor The prime contractor who contracts for the construction of an entire building or project, rather than just a portion of the work. The general contractor hires subcontractors (e.g., plumbing, electrical, etc.), coordinates all work, and is responsible for payment to subcontractors.

general partner A member of a partnership who has authority to bind the partnership. A general partner also shares in the profits and losses of the partnership. See also *limited partnership*.

graduated lease A lease, generally long term in nature, that provides that the rent will vary depending on future contingencies, such as a periodic appraisal, the tenant's gross income, or simply the passage of time.

grant To bestow or transfer an interest in real property by deed or other instrument, either the fee or a lesser interest, such as an easement.

grantee One to whom a grant is made.

grantor The person making the grant.

gross absorption A measure of the total square feet leased over a specified period of time with no consideration given to space vacated in the same geographic area during the same time period. See also *net absorption*.

gross building area The total floor area of the building measuring from the outer surface of exterior walls and windows and including all vertical penetrations (e.g., elevator shafts, etc.) and basement space.

gross lease A lease in which the tenant pays a flat sum for rent out of which the landlord must pay all expenses such as taxes, insurance, maintenance, utilities, etc.

ground rent Rent paid to the owner for use of land, normally on which to build a building. Generally, the arrangement is that of a long-term lease (e.g., 99 years) with the lessor retaining title to the land.

guarantor One who makes a guaranty. See also *guaranty*.

guaranty Agreement whereby the guarantor undertakes collaterally to ensure satisfaction of the debt of another or perform the obligation of another if and when the debtor fails to do so. Differs from a surety agreement in that there is a separate and distinct contract rather than a joint undertaking with the principal. See also *guarantor*.

H

hard cost The cost of actually constructing the improvements (i.e., construction costs). See also *soft cost*.

highest and best use The use of land or buildings that will bring the greatest economic return over a given time that is physically possible, appropriately supported, financially feasible.

high rise In the central business district, this could mean a building higher than 25 stories above ground level, but in suburban submarkets, it generally refers to buildings higher than 7 or 8 stories.

hold over tenant A tenant retaining possession of the leased premises after the expiration of a lease.

HVAC The acronym for heating, ventilating, and air-conditioning.

I

improvements In the context of leasing, the term typically refers to the improvements made to or inside a building but may include any permanent structure or other development, such as a street, sidewalks, utilities, etc. See also *leasehold improvements* and *tenant improvements*.

indirect costs Development costs, other than material and labor costs, that are directly related to the construction of improvements, including administrative and office expenses, commissions, architectural, engineering, and financing costs.

inventory The total amount of rentable square feet of existing and any forthcoming space (whether it be a tenant vacating space or new buildings coming on the market) in a given category; for example, all warehouse space in a specified submarket. Inventory refers to all space within a certain proscribed market without regard to its availability or condition, and categories can include all types of leased space such as office, flex, retail, and warehouse space.

J

judgment The final decision of a court resolving a dispute and determining the rights and obligations of the parties. Money judgments, when recorded, become a lien on real property of the defendant.

judgment lien An encumbrance that arises by law when a judgment for the recovery of money attaches to the debtor's real estate. See also *lien*.

just compensation Compensation that is fair to both the owner and the public when property is taken for public use through condemnation (eminent domain). The theory is that in order to be "just," the property owner should be no richer or poorer than before the taking.

L

landlord's lien A type of lien that can be created by contract or by operation of law. Some examples are (1) a contractual landlord's lien as might be found in a lease agreement; (2) a statutory landlord's lien, and (3) landlord's remedy of distress (or right of distraint), which is not truly a lien but has a similar effect. See also *lien*.

landlord's lien or warrant A warrant from a landlord to levy on a tenant's personal property (e.g., furniture, etc.) and to sell this property at a public sale to compel payment of the rent or the observance of some other stipulation in the lease.

lease An agreement whereby the owner of real property (i.e., landlord/lessor) gives the right of possession to another (i.e., tenant/lessee) for a specified period of time (i.e., term) and for a specified consideration (i.e., rent).

lease agreement The formal legal document entered into between a landlord and a tenant to reflect the terms of the negotiations between them; that is, the lease terms have been negotiated and agreed on, and the agreement has been reduced to writing. It constitutes the entire agreement between the parties and sets forth their basic legal rights.

lease commencement date The date usually constitutes the commencement of the term of the lease for all purposes, whether or not the tenant has actually taken possession, so long as beneficial occupancy is possible. In reality, there could be other agreements, such as an early occupancy agreement, that have an impact on this strict definition.

leasehold improvements Improvements made to the leased premises by or for a tenant. Generally, especially in new space, part of the negotiations will include in some detail the improvements to be made in the leased premises by landlord. See also *tenant improvements.*

legal description A geographical description identifying a parcel of land by government survey, metes and bounds, or lot numbers of a recorded plat including a description of any portion thereof that is subject to an easement or reservation.

legal owner The term is in technical contrast to equitable owner. The legal owner has title to the property, although the title may actually carry no rights to the property other than as a lien. See also *lien.*

letter of attornment A letter from the grantor to a tenant, stating that a property has been sold and directing rent to be paid to the grantee (buyer). See also *attorn.*

letter of credit A commitment by a bank or other person, made at the request of a customer, that the issuer will honor drafts or other demands for payment on full compliance with the conditions specified in the letter of credit. Letters of credit are often used in place of cash deposited with the landlord in satisfying the security deposit provisions of a lease.

letter of intent A preliminary agreement stating the proposed terms for a final contract. They can be binding or nonbinding. This is the threshold issue in most litigation concerning letters of intent. The parties should always consult their respective legal counsel before signing any letter of intent.

lien A claim or encumbrance against property used to secure a debt, charge, or the performance of some act. Includes liens acquired by contract or by operation of law. Note that all liens are encumbrances, but all encumbrances are not liens.

lien waiver (waiver of liens) A waiver of mechanic's lien rights, signed by a general contractor and his subcontractors, that is often required before the general contractor can receive a draw under the payment provisions of a construction contract. May also be required before the owner can receive a draw on a construction loan.

like-kind property A term used in an exchange of property held for productive use in a trade or business or for investment. Unless cash is received, the tax consequences of the exchange are postponed pursuant to Section 1031 of the Internal Revenue Code.

limited partnership A type of partnership, created under state law, comprised of one or more general partners who manage the business and who are personally liable for partnership debts, and one or more special or limited partners who contribute capital and share in profits but who take no part in running the business and incur no liability over and above the amount contributed. See also *general partner*.

listing agreement An agreement between the owner of a property and a real estate broker giving the broker the authorization to attempt to sell or lease the property at a certain price and terms in return for a commission, set fee, or other form of compensation. See also *exclusive listing agreement.*

long-term lease In most markets, this refers to a lease whose term is at least three years from initial signing until the date of expiration or renewal option.

lot Generally, one of several contiguous parcels of land making up a fractional part or subdivision of a block, the boundaries of which are shown on recorded maps and *plats.*

low rise A building with fewer than four stories above ground level.

lump-sum contract A type of construction contract requiring the general contractor to complete a building or project for a fixed cost normally established by competitive bidding. The contractor absorbs any loss or retains any profit.

M

maker One who creates or executes a promissory note and promises to pay the note when it becomes due.

market rent The rental income that a property would command on the open market with a landlord and a tenant ready and willing to consummate a lease in the ordinary course of business; indicated by the rents that landlords were willing to accept and tenants were willing to pay in recent lease transactions for comparable space.

market study A forecast of future demand for a certain type of real estate project that includes an estimate of the square footage that can be absorbed and the rents that can be charged. Also called *marketability study.*

marketable title A title that is free from encumbrances and can be readily marketed (i.e., sold) to a reasonably intelligent purchaser who is well informed of the facts and willing to accept such title while exercising ordinary business prudence. See also *encumbrance.*

market value The highest price a property would command in a competitive and open market under all conditions requisite to a fair sale with the buyer and seller each acting prudently and knowledgeably in the ordinary course of trade.

master lease A primary lease that controls subsequent leases and that may cover more property than subsequent leases. An executive suite operation is a good example in that a primary lease is signed with the landlord, and then individual offices within the leased premises are leased to other individuals or companies.

mechanic's lien A claim created by state statutes for the purpose of securing priority of payment of the price and value of work performed and materials furnished in constructing, repairing, or improving a building or other structure, and that attaches to the land as well as to the buildings and improvements thereon.

metes and bounds The boundary lines of land, with their terminal points and angles, described by listing the compass directions and distances of the boundaries. Originally, metes referred to distance and bounds referred to direction.

mid-rise A building with between 4 and 8 stories above ground level; although in a central business district, this might extend to buildings up to 25 stories.

mixed-use Space within a building or project providing for more than one use (i.e., a loft or apartment project with retail, an apartment building with office space, an office building with retail space).

mortgage A written instrument creating an interest in real estate and that provides security for the performance of a duty or the payment of a debt. The borrower (i.e., mortgagor) retains possession and use of the property.

N

net absorption The square feet leased in a specific geographic area over a fixed period of time after deducting space vacated in the same area during the same period. See also *gross absorption*.

net lease A lease in which there is a provision for the tenant to pay, in addition to rent, certain costs associated with the operation of the property. These costs may include property taxes, insurance, repairs, utilities, and maintenance. There are also "NN" (double net) and "NNN" (triple net) leases. The difference between the three is the degree to which the tenant is responsible for operating costs. See also *gross lease.*

net rentable area The floor area of a building that remains after the square footage represented by vertical penetrations, such as elevator shafts, etc., has been deducted. Common areas and mechanical rooms are included, and there are no deductions made for necessary columns and projections of the building. (This is by the Building Owners and Managers Association, or BOMA, standard.)

net square footage (SF) The space required for a function or staff position. Also see *circulation factor* and *usable square footage.*

noncompete clause A clause that can be inserted into a lease specifying that the business of the tenant is exclusive in the property and that no other tenant operating the same or similar type of business can occupy space in the building. This clause benefits service-oriented businesses desiring exclusive access to the building's population (i.e., travel agent, deli, etc.).

nonrecourse loan A loan that bars a lender from seeking a deficiency judgment against a borrower in the event of default. The borrower is not personally liable if the value of the collateral for the loan falls below the amount required to repay the loan.

normal wear and tear The deterioration or loss in value caused by the tenant's normal and reasonable use. In many leases the tenant is not responsible for "normal wear and tear."

O

open space An unimproved area of land or water, or containing only such improvements as are appropriate to the use and enjoyment of the open area, and dedicated for public or private use or enjoyment or for the use and enjoyment of owners and occupants of land adjoining or neighboring such open spaces.

operating cost escalation Although there are many variations of escalation clauses, all are intended to adjust rents by reference to external standards, such as published indexes, negotiated wage levels, or expenses related to the ownership and operation of buildings. During the past 30 years, landlords have developed the custom of separating the base rent for the occupancy of the leased premises from escalation rent. This technique enables the landlord to better ensure that the net rent to be received under the lease will not be reduced by the normal costs of operating and maintaining the property. The landlord's definition of operating expenses is likely to be broad, covering most costs of operation of the building. Most landlords pass through proper and customary charges, but in the hands of an overly aggressive landlord, these clauses can operate to impose obligations that the tenant would not willingly or knowingly accept.

operating expenses The actual costs associated with operating a property, including maintenance, repairs, management, utilities, taxes, and insurance. A landlord's definition of operating expenses is likely to be quite broad, covering most aspects of operating the building.

operating expense escalation Although there are many variations of operating expense escalation clauses, all are intended to adjust rents by reference to external standards, such as published indexes, negotiated wage levels, or expenses related to the ownership and operation of buildings.

P

parking ratio or index The intent of this ratio is to provide a uniform method of expressing the amount of parking that is available at a given building. Dividing the total rentable square footage of a building by the building's total number of parking spaces provides the amount of rentable square feet per each individual parking space (expressed as 1/xxx or 1 per xxx). Dividing 1,000 by the previous result provides the ratio of parking spaces available per each 1,000 rentable square feet (expressed as x per 1,000).

partial taking The taking of part (a portion) of an owner's property under the laws of eminent domain.

pass throughs Refers to the tenant's pro rata share of operating expenses (i.e., taxes, utilities, repairs) paid in addition to the base rent.

percentage lease Refers to a provision of the lease calling for the landlord to be paid a percentage of the tenant's gross sales as a component of rent. There is usually a base rent amount to which "percentage" rent is then added. This type of clause is most often found in retail leases.

performance bond A surety bond posted by a contractor guaranteeing full performance of a contract with the proceeds to be used to complete the contract or compensate for the owner's loss in the event of nonperformance.

plat (plat map) Map of a specific area, such as a subdivision, that shows the boundaries of individual parcels of land (e.g., lots) together with streets and easements.

power of sale Clause inserted in a mortgage or deed of trust giving the mortgagee (or trustee) the right and power, on default in the payment of the debt secured, to advertise and sell the property at public auction.

precast concrete Concrete components (i.e., walls) of a building that are fabricated at a plant site and then shipped to the site of construction.

preleased Refers to space in a proposed building that has been leased before the start of construction or in advance of the issuance of a certificate of occupancy.

prime space This typically refers to first generation (new) space that is currently available for lease and that has never before been occupied by a tenant.

prime tenant The major tenant in a building or the major or anchor tenant in a shopping center serving to attract other, smaller tenants into adjacent space because of the customer traffic generated.

pro rata Proportionately; according to measure, interest, or liability. In the case of a tenant, the proportionate share of expenses for the maintenance and operation of the property. See also *common area* and *operating expenses.*

punch list An itemized list, typically prepared by the architect or construction manager, documenting incomplete or unsatisfactory items after the contractor has notified the owner that the tenant space is substantially complete.

Q

quitclaim deed A deed operating as a release that is intended to pass any title, interest, or claim that the grantor may have in the property, but not containing any warranty or professing that such title is valid.

R

raw land Unimproved land that remains in its natural state.

raw space Unimproved *shell space* in a building.

REO (real estate owned) Real estate that has come to be owned by a lender, including real estate taken to satisfy a debt. Includes real estate acquired by lenders through foreclosure or in settlement of some other obligation.

real property Land and generally whatever is erected or affixed to the land, such as buildings and fences, and including light fixtures, plumbing and heating fixtures, or other items that would be personal property if not attached.

recapture (1) When the IRS recovers the tax benefit of a deduction or a credit previously taken by a taxpayer, which is often a factor in foreclosure since there is a forgiveness of debt. (2) As used in leases, a clause giving the lessor a percentage of profits above a fixed amount of rent; or in a percentage lease, a clause granting the landlord a right to terminate the lease if the tenant fails to realize minimum sales.

recourse The right of a lender, in the event of a default by the borrower, to recover against the personal assets of a party that is secondarily liable for the debt (e.g., endorser or guarantor).

rehab An extensive renovation of a building or project that is intended to cure obsolescence of such building or project.

renewal option A clause giving a tenant the right to extend the term of a lease, usually for a stated period of time and at a rent amount as provided for in the option language.

rent Compensation or fee paid, usually periodically (i.e., monthly rent payments), for the occupancy and use of any rental property, land, buildings, equipment, etc.

rent commencement date The date on which a tenant begins paying rent. The dynamics of a marketplace will dictate whether this date coincides with the lease commencement date or if it commences months later (i.e., in a weak market, the tenant may be granted several months free rent). It will never begin before the lease commencement date.

rentable square footage Rentable square footage equals the usable square footage plus the tenant's pro rata share of the building common areas, such as lobbies, public corridors, and restrooms. The pro rata share, often referred to as the rentable/usable (R/U) factor, will typically fall in a range of 1.10 to 1.16, depending on the particular building. Typically, a full-floor occupancy will have an R/U factor of 1.10, while a partial floor occupancy will have an R/U factor of 1.12 to 1.16 times the usable area.

rentable/usable ratio That number obtained when the total rentable area in a building is divided by the usable area in the building. The inverse of this ratio describes the proportion of space that an occupant can expect to actually utilize/physically occupy.

rental concession Concessions a landlord may offer a tenant in order to secure their tenancy. While rental abatement is one form of a concession, there are many others, such as increased tenant improvement allowance, signage, lower than market rental rates, moving allowances, and many others. See also *abatement.*

rent-up period That period of time, following construction of a new building, when tenants are actively being sought and the project is approaching its stabilized occupancy.

representation agreement An agreement between the owner of a property and a real estate broker giving the broker the authorization to attempt to sell or lease the property at a certain price and terms in return for a commission, set fee, or other form of compensation. See also *exclusive listing agreement.*

Request for Proposal (RFP) The formalized Request for Proposal represents a compilation of the many considerations that a tenant might have and should be customized to reflect their specific needs. Just as the building's standard form lease document represents the landlord's "wish list," the RFP serves in that same capacity for the tenant.

right of first refusal See *first refusal right.*

S

sale-leaseback An arrangement by which the owner occupant of a property agrees to sell all or part of the property to an investor and then lease it back and continue to occupy space as a tenant. Although the lease technically follows the sale, both will have been agreed to as part of the same transaction.

second mortgage A mortgage on property that ranks below a first mortgage in priority. Properties may have two, three, or more mortgages, deeds of trust, or land contracts as liens at the same time. Legal sequence priority, indicated by the date of recording, determines the designation first, second, third, etc.

second generation or secondary space Refers to previously occupied space that becomes available for lease, either directly from the landlord or as sublease space. See also *first generation space.*

security deposit A deposit of money by a tenant to a landlord to secure performance of a lease. This deposit can also take the form of a letter of credit or other financial instrument.

seisen (seizen) Possession of real property under claim of freehold estate. This term originally referred to the completion of feudal investiture by which a tenant was admitted into the feud and performed the rights of homage and fealty. Presently it has come to mean possession under a legal right (usually a fee interest). As the old doctrine of corporeal investiture is no longer in force, the delivery of a deed gives *seisin* in law.

setback The distance from a curb, property line, or other reference point, within which building is prohibited.

setback ordinance Setback requirements are normally provided for by ordinances or building codes. Provisions of a zoning ordinance regulate the distance from the lot line to the point where improvements may be constructed.

shell space The interior condition of the tenant's usable square footage when it is without improvements or finishes. While existing improvements and finishes can be removed, thus returning space in an older building to its "shell" condition, the term most commonly refers to the condition of the usable square footage after completion of the building's shell construction but prior to the build-out of the tenant's space. Shell construction typically denotes the floor, windows, walls, and roof of an enclosed premises and may include some HVAC, electrical, or plumbing improvements but not demising walls or interior space partitioning. In a new multitenant building, the common area improvements, such as lobbies, restrooms, and exit corridors may also be included in the shell construction. With a newly constructed office building, there will often be a distinction between improvements above and below the ceiling grid. In a retail project, all or a portion of the floor slab is often installed along with the tenant improvements so as to better accommodate tenant specific underfloor plumbing requirements.

site analysis The study of a specific parcel of land that takes into account the surrounding area and is meant to determine its suitability for a specific use or purpose.

site development The installation of all necessary improvements (i.e., installment of utilities, grading, etc.) made to a site before a building or project can be constructed on such site.

site plan A detailed plan that depicts the location of improvements on a parcel of land and that also contains all the information required by the zoning ordinance.

slab The exposed wearing surface laid over the structural support beams of a building to form the floor(s) of the building or laid slab-on-grade in the case of a nonstructural, ground-level concrete slab.

soft cost That portion of an equity investment other than the actual cost of the improvements themselves (i.e., architectural and engineering fees, commissions, etc.) and that may be tax-deductible in the first year. See also *hard cost.*

space plan A graphic representation of a tenant's space requirements, showing wall and door locations and room sizes, and sometimes including furniture layouts. A preliminary space plan will be prepared for a prospective tenant at any number of different properties, and this serves as a "test-fit" to help the tenant determine which property will best meet its requirements. When the tenant has selected a building of choice, a final space plan is prepared that speaks to all of the landlord and tenant objectives and is then approved by both parties. It must be sufficiently detailed to allow an accurate estimate of the construction costs. This final space plan will often become an exhibit to any lease negotiated between the parties.

special assessment Any special charge levied against real property for public improvements (e.g., sidewalks, streets, water and sewer, etc.) that benefit the assessed property.

specific performance A requirement compelling one of the parties to perform or carry out the provisions of a contract into which it has entered.

speculative space Any tenant space that has not been leased before the start of construction on a new building. See also first generation space.

step-up lease (graded lease) A lease specifying set increases in rent at set intervals during the term of the lease.

straight lease (flat lease) A lease specifying the same, a fixed amount, of rent that is to be paid periodically during the entire term of the lease. This is typically paid out in monthly installments.

strip center Any shopping area, generally with common parking, that comprises a row of stores but is smaller than the neighborhood center anchored by a grocery store.

subcontractor A contractor working under and being paid by the general contractor. Often a specialist in nature, such as an electrical contractor, cement contractor, etc.

subdivision plat A detailed drawing that depicts the manner in which a parcel of land has been divided into two or more lots. It contains engineering considerations and other information required by the local authority.

subordination agreement As used in a lease, the tenant generally accepts the leased premises subject to any recorded mortgage or deed of trust lien and all existing recorded restrictions, and the landlord is often given the power to subordinate the tenant's interest to any first mortgage or deed of trust lien subsequently placed on the leased premises.

surety One who at the request of another, and for the purpose of securing to him or her a benefit, voluntarily binds himself or herself to be obligated for the debt or obligation of another. Although the term includes guarantor and the terms are commonly, though mistakenly, used interchangeably, surety differs from guarantor in a variety of respects.

surface rights A right or easement granted with mineral rights, enabling the possessor of the mineral rights to drill or mine through the surface.

survey The process by which a parcel of land is measured and its boundaries and contents ascertained.

T

taking A common synonym for condemnation or any actual or material interference with private property rights, but it is not essential that there be physical seizure or appropriation.

tax base The assessed valuation of all the real property that lies within the jurisdiction of a taxing authority, which is then multiplied by the tax rate or mill levy to determine the amount of tax due.

tax lien A statutory lien, existing in favor of the state or municipality, for nonpayment of property taxes that attaches only to the property on which the taxes are unpaid.

tax roll A list or record containing the descriptions of all land parcels located within the county, the names of the owners or those receiving the tax bill, assessed values, and tax amounts.

tenant (lessee) One who rents real estate from another and holds an estate by virtue of a lease.

tenant at will One who holds possession of premises by permission of the owner or landlord, the characteristics of which are an uncertain duration (i.e., without a fixed term) and the right of either party to terminate on proper notice.

tenant improvements Improvements made to the leased premises by or for a tenant. Generally, especially in new space, part of the negotiations will include in some detail the improvements to be made in the leased premises by the landlord. See also *leasehold improvements* and *workletter.*

tenant improvement (TI) allowance or workletter Defines the fixed amount of money contributed by the landlord toward tenant improvements. The tenant pays any of the costs that exceed this amount. Also commonly referred to as *tenant finish allowance.*

"time is of the essence" Means that performance by one party within the period specified in the contract is essential to require performance by the other party.

title The means whereby the owner of lands has the just and full possession of real property.

title insurance A policy issued by a title company after searching the title, which insures against loss resulting from defects of title to a specifically described parcel of real property or from the enforcement of liens existing against it at the time the title policy is issued.

title search A review of all recorded documents affecting a specific piece of property to determine the present condition of title.

total inventory The total amount of square footage of a type of property (i.e., office, industrial, retail, etc.) within a geographical area, whether vacant or occupied. This normally includes owner-occupied space.

trade fixtures Personal property that is attached to a structure (i.e., the walls of the leased premises) that are used in the business. Since this property is part of the business and not deemed to be part of the real estate, it is typically removable on lease termination.

triple net (NNN) rent A lease in which the tenant pays, in addition to rent, certain costs associated with a leased property, which may include property taxes, insurance premiums, repairs, utilities, and maintenance. There are also *net leases* and NN (double-net) leases, depending on the degree to which the tenant is responsible for operating costs. See also *gross lease*.

turn key project The construction of a project in which a third party, usually a developer or general contractor, is responsible for the total completion of a building (including construction and interior design) or the construction of tenant improvements to the customized requirements and specifications of a future owner or tenant.

U

under construction When construction has started but the *certificate of occupancy* has not yet been issued.

under contract A property for which the seller has accepted the buyer's offer to purchase is referred to as being "under contract." Generally, the prospective buyer is given a certain period of time in which to perform its due diligence and finalize financing arrangements. During the period of time the property is under contract, the seller is precluded from entertaining offers from other buyers.

unencumbered Describes title to property that is free of liens and any other encumbrances. Free and clear. See also *encumbrances.*

unimproved land Most commonly refers to land without improvements or buildings but can also mean land in its natural state. See also *raw land.*

use The specific purpose for which a parcel of land or a building is intended to be used or for which it has been designed or arranged.

usable square footage Usable square footage is the area contained within the demising walls of the tenant space. Total usable square footage equals the net square footage times the circulation factor. Also see *circulation factor* and *net square footage.*

V

vacancy factor The amount of gross revenue that pro forma income statements anticipate will be lost because of vacancies, often expressed as a percentage of the total rentable square footage available in a building or project.

vacancy rate The total amount of available space compared to the total inventory of space and expressed as a percentage. This is calculated by multiplying the vacant space times 100 and then dividing it by the total inventory.

vacant space Refers to existing tenant space currently being marketed for lease. This excludes space available for sublease.

variance Refers to permission that allows a property owner to depart from the literal requirements of a zoning ordinance that, because of special circumstances, cause a unique hardship. Included would be such things as the particular physical surroundings, shape, or topographical condition of the property, and when compliance would result in a practical difficulty and would deprive the owner of the reasonable use of the property.

W

warranty of possession This is the old "quiet enjoyment" paragraph, which of course had nothing to do with noise in and around the leased premises. It provides a warranty by a landlord that he or she has the legal ability to convey the possession of the premises to the tenant; the landlord does not warrant that he or she owns the land. This is the essence of the landlord's agreement and the tenant's obligation to pay rent. This means that if the landlord breaches this warranty, it constitutes an actual or constructive eviction.

weighted average rental rates The mean proportion or medial sum made out of the unequal rental rates in two or more buildings within a market area.

workletter A list of the building standard items that the landlord will contribute as part of the tenant improvements. Examples of the building standard items typically identified include style and type of doors, lineal feet of partitions, type and quantity of lights, quality of floor coverings, number of telephone and electrical outlets, etc. The workletter often carries a dollar value but is contrasted with a fixed dollar tenant improvement allowance that can be used at the tenant's discretion. See also *leasehold improvements* and *tenant improvements*.

working drawings The set of plans for a building or project that comprise the contract documents that indicate the precise manner in which a project is to be built. This set of plans includes a set of specifications for the building or project.

Z

zoning The division of a city or town into zones and the application of regulations having to do with the structural, architectural design, and intended use of buildings within such designated zone (i.e., a tenant needing manufacturing space would look for a building located within an area zoned for manufacturing).

zoning ordinance Refers to the set of laws and regulations, generally, at the city or county level, controlling the use of land and construction of improvements in a given area or zone.

Share the message!

Bulk discounts
Discounts start at only 10 copies and range from 30% to 55% off
retail price based on quantity.

Custom publishing
Private label a cover with your organization's name and logo.
Or, tailor information to your needs with a custom pamphlet
that highlights specific chapters.

Ancillaries
Workshop outlines, videos, and other products are available on
select titles.

Dynamic speakers
Engaging authors are available to share their expertise and insight
at your event.

**Call Dearborn Trade Special Sales at
1-800-621-9621, ext. 4444,
or e-mail trade@dearborn.com**

Dearborn™
Trade Publishing
A **Kaplan Professional** Company